Introducti

L ying between the Vale of Clwyd and the S little known wild, beautiful, unspoilt uplan(walkers and tourists alike as they head to crow ... . is a large undulating upland plateau containing an expansive heather moorland, now designated Open Access land, and several large lakes, most notably Llyn Brenig, with its Visitor Centre and nearby Alwen reservoir. On its eastern side is Clocaenog Forest – an important habitat for red squirrels – and elsewhere are delightful open hills.

The area has been occupied by man since about 5700 BC. when a better climate and woodland habitat first attracted nomadic hunters. It contains important Bronze Age ceremonial and burial sites and Iron-Age hillforts. From the Middle Ages to the 19thC black cattle, often from Anglesey, were grazed on the upland pastures before being taken by drovers to distant markets in England. Cerrigydrudion is the largest settlement, lying on an important drovers route and the original 18thC London-Holyhead turnpike coach road, later improved by Thomas Telford, now the A5. In 1854, George Borrow, the eminent traveller and writer of 'Wild Wales' walked this way.

Easily accessible, the area offers excellent walking with a great sense of space and superb views, especially of the mountains of Snowdonia from the western part of the area. The 22 circular walks in this updated third edition of the book explore its moorland, hills, river valleys, lakes, woods and forests. They follow old drovers' roads and visit ancient communities and sites of historical interest, whilst providing an insight into the area's history. They include sections of the waymarked Hiraethog Trail linking the area's scattered villages, the popular circuit of Llyn Brenig and the Alwen Trail.

The routes, which range from a 2½ mile Archaeological Trail to an exhilarating 10½ mile moorland challenge, follow public rights of way, permissive paths or cross Open Access land. A key feature is that most individual routes, as well as containing shorter walk options, can easily be linked to provide longer and more challenging day walks, if required. Be suitably equipped, especially on the more remote exposed moorland routes. Walking boots are recommended, along with appropriate clothing to protect against the elements. Please remember that the condition of paths can vary according to season and weather. Refer any rights of way problems encountered to the relevant local authority (see page 40)

Each walk has a detailed map and description which enables the route to be followed without difficulty, but be aware that changes in detail can occur at any time. The location of each walk is shown on the back cover and a summary of their key features is also given. This includes an estimated walking time, but allow more time to enjoy the scenery. Please observe the country code. *Enjoy your walking!*

WALK I

AFON CLYWEDOG & FOEL GANOL

DESCRIPTION A delightful 4 mile walk exploring the valleys and hills near Cyffylliog - a secluded old settlement lying in the wooded Clywedog valley only 4 miles west of Ruthin – offering extensive views. The route, which is part of a waymarked Mynydd Hiraethog circuit, follows a lovely section of the Clywedog river, then rises up an attractive side valley to follow a high-level country road along the northern slopes of Foel Ganol. It then descends to Cyffylliog by either a delightful green track past Llyn Gloyw and road (**A**) or by upland pasture (**B**). Allow about 2½ hours. The Red Lion, a traditional village inn offering good food and drink, makes a good finish to the walk.

START Cyffylliog [SJ 060578].

DIRECTIONS From Ruthin take the B5105 towards Cerrigydrudion and just after passing Llanfwrog church, take the road signposted to Cyffylliog. Go through Bontuchel and over the river into Cyffylliog where there is limited roadside parking.

*C*yffylliog *is thought to date to the 12thC. According to folklore, the parish was haunted by mischievous fairies, who used to take horses from their stables and ride them all night, returning them dirty and exhausted. So, it is best to explore this area during daylight hours – just in case!*

From the centre of the village, take the road signposted to Nantglyn. Soon you pass the old Georgian 'hearse house' and the simple Church of St Mary dating from the 15thC. A little further, take the signposted Brenig Way path on the right by Hyfrydle to cross a footbridge over the Afon Clywedog. Follow the path briefly by the river then beneath a house and across its access track by a bridge over the river to a gate. Follow the delightful scenic path above the river. Later, after a gate the waymarked path continues a little way from the river, goes through another gate, crosses a stream, then descends a stony access track from a nearby cottage. After a gate, as the track descends towards the river, angle RIGHT along a wide path to a gate. Continue with the waymarked path through a section of cleared forest, rising steadily up an old track initially above the fast-flowing river – *with wind turbines becoming visible above the conifers further down the valley* – later descending to a track T- junction. Turn RIGHT up the track and follow it northwards along the top of the steep slope past replanted deciduous woodland to a stile/gate – *with good views across the Concwest valley.*

2 Here, you leave the waymarked trail and go along the narrow green track ahead on a long steady climb across the western slopes of Foel Uchaf to a road. Turn RIGHT along the attractive quiet upland country road across the northern slopes of Foel Ganol – *providing steady walking and extensive open views: north towards Denbigh, the northern Clwydian Range, and the coast at Rhyl; and ahead to the central Clwydian Range, extending south from Moel y Parc with its TV transmitter mast to the highest point-Moel Famau, with its distinctive ruined Jubilee Tower – and on to Moel Fenlli, with its Iron-Age hillfort.* After ¾ mile, at a road junction just before a former farm, keep with the right fork, bending south with the road.

3 Here you have a choice of return routes. For **Route A** continue along the road, then at a cattle-grid, cross a stile on the left. Now follow the signposted path along a green track across the open upland pasture of Moel y Fron – *with extensive views west.* As the delightful track begins to descend and passes Llyn Gloyw, new views unfold of the Clwydian Range and the Llantisilio Mountains. Eventually the track ends at a road. Follow the road down into Cyffylliog.

For **Route B**, after about 60 yards, take a signposted path over a stile on the right by a gate and follow a green track along the field edge parallel with the road. Soon the track descends to a gate and continues down to Foel Ganol cottage. At its far garden corner, go through a gate and continue ahead down a large field to go through a waymarked gate-

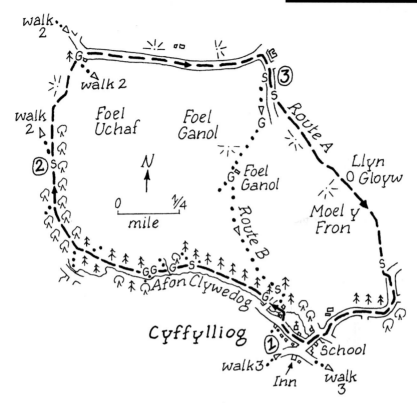

Foel Uchaf

Foel Ganol

Foel Ganol

N

0 ¼ mile

Llyn O Gloyw

Route A

Route B

Moel y Fron

Afon Clywedog

Cyffylliog

School

Inn

walk 2

walk 2

walk 2

walk 3

walk 3

way in the bottom corner. Go down the next field, parallel with the tree boundary on your right, and on to cross a stile at the left-hand wood corner. Follow the path down through the trees to pass behind a house and down through the garden edge to join your outward route.

Hearse House

WALK 2
CLYWEDOG RESERVOIR & FOEL UCHAF

DESCRIPTION A 9 mile stretched figure of eight undulating walk (**A**) featuring attractive wooded river valleys, open hills, forest, a small hidden attractive upland fishing reservoir and excellent views. The route also offers an alternative 4½ (**B**) or 3¾ (**C**) mile walk around Foel Uchaf. The main walk follows part of a way-marked Hiraethog Trail path along the attractive Clywedog and Concwest valleys, before rising in stages on minor roads and open/forestry tracks to reach the Clywedog reservoir at 1377 feet/420 metres. The return follows a waymarked byway past the small hill of Bryn Ocyn, then a choice of routes to rejoin your outward route. From the Concwest valley, you follow an attractive upland road, then rise to cross the eastern slopes of Foel Uchaf before descending back into the Clywedog valley. Allow about 4½ hours. An alternative 3 mile walk can be followed from the reservoir itself, starting at point 4, then taking either route **a** or **b** to join the main route back. Follow minor roads from Saron past wind turbines and through the forest then turn left along a stony track (waymarked byway/Brenig Way) to the reservoir.
START Cyffylliog [SJ 060578] See Walk 1.

I Follow instructions for the first section of Walk 1. (For **Walk C** then continue ahead up the green track to join the returning main route at point **5** by the road.

2 (For **Walks A** and **B**, go through a gate ahead. Continue ahead across the large sloping field, soon passing through an area of gorse, to a fallen waymark post ahead. Here bear LEFT to cross a stile in a fence. The path now follows the Afon Concwest, along the bottom edge of a delightful area of predominantly oak woodland, past an old inclined track, over two stiles to a road. (For **Walk B**, turn right and follow the road to point **5**.)

3 Turn LEFT and follow the road up to a junction, then turn RIGHT up the side road. After a while the road levels out and passes Bryn-ochan farm. At Penrhos the road bends left to the larger house of Boced. Continue along the rougher road – *enjoying panoramic views across the Clywedog valley to the Clwydian Range* – shortly descending to a cattle grid at a junction of stony tracks. Follow the track ahead down to a gate. The delightful track continues west along the top edge of the Clywedog valley – *with wind turbines above the forest skyline ahead.* When it splits, go up the RIGHT fork to a gate. The track rises steadily across the hillside planted with new trees, later passing a small quarry and bending right

Bryn

Clywedog Reservoir

through mature trees. Shortly it bends left past a side track on the right and continues to the Clywedog reservoir – *popular with wildfowl and fishermen. At the car park is a large plaque commemorating the restoration of the reservoir for fly-fishing in 2005. From its eastern end a path angles past a seat towards the dam, with a good view of the reservoir. Fishermen only beyond this point.*

4 From the end of the car park opposite the side track heading north take a near-by white waymarked narrow stony track angling NE. Follow it through heather and open forest to a crossroad of tracks. Follow the waymarked track ahead through the forest to a gate into upland pasture. Continue with the delightful green track beside the fence beneath Bryn Ochan past the forest. Shortly you have a choice. For **route a** go to a stile/gate (Clwydian Way) in the fence corner. Follow the green track across and down the upland pasture to a stile and on through

4

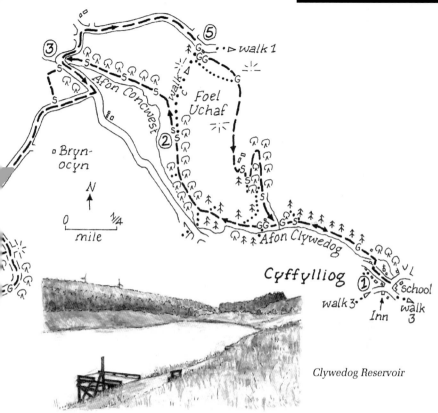

Clywedog Reservoir

gates to rejoin your outward route at the road by Boced. For **route b** follow the waymarked bridleway from a nearby stile/small gate down the edge of the large field to a stile/gate and on to the junction of stony tracks met earlier. For both routes follow your outward route past Bryn-ochan farm. Later cross a stile on the left and head straight down the steep field. At the bottom edge above bracken, a path descends a few yards, then bears RIGHT down to a stile and the road at point **3**. Follow it up to a junction. Turn RIGHT, past a side road, and continue up the attractive quiet upland country road.

5 After passing another side road, take a signposted path through a gate on your right by Foel Ucha's access track. Go through a gate by the corrugated barn and another ahead, then up the middle of the large field to a small gate in the top corner onto the bend of the track at a prominent viewpoint – *with superb views looking north to Denbigh and down the Vale of Clwyd to the coast.* Follow the track south across Foel Uchaf, soon descending steadily – *with good views of the Clywedog valley and the southern Clwydian Range.* Just after it bends towards the farm entrance take a signposted path over a stile on the right. Follow the path down past Scots pines to another stile. Just beyond turn LEFT down a green track, soon bending sharp right down between areas of young trees. When the track briefly rises continue more or less ahead following an old sunken track down to a stile. (If the path is still blocked by young trees, which I have reported, continue down the green track to join your outward route earlier.) Go down the field to a stile near a cottage and down its access track to join your outward route.

5

WALK 3

PINCYN LLYS FROM CYFFYLLIOG

DESCRIPTION A 7¾ mile walk (**A**) from a secluded village with its medieval church and country inn through undulating upland pasture and forest to the top of Pincyn Llys, with its unusual stone monument and panoramic views. Allow about 4 hours. A shorter 3¼ mile walk (**B**) is included.
START Cyffylliog [SJ 060578] See Walk I.

Pincyn Llys is a part-forested hill (1358 feet)/414 metres) lying between Cyffylliog and Clocaenog. The monument was erected in 1830 by the Second Lord Bagot to commemorate the planting of forest. A later inscription records that the plantation was felled during and after the 1914-18 war, and Clocaenog Forest was created in 1930. The monument stands at the corner of an ancient earthwork known as 'Llys y Frenhines' – 'The Queen's Court House' – from which a boulder shaped like an armchair called 'Cader y Frenhines' ('The Queen's Chair') was removed to Lord Bagot's residence at Pool Park in 1804.

I Take the minor road leading east from the Red Lion, past a phone box. Follow it for about 1¼ miles. Shortly after passing Tyddyn-Bach, turn RIGHT up a track to a stile/gate. Continue up the track, and immediately after it bends left, take a path on the right up the edge of the wood to rejoin the forestry track. Follow the waymarked path opposite up through the conifers to a stile. Go ahead up the large field, past a solitary tree and on to a stile in a fence corner – *with a good view of the Clwydian Range.* Follow the waymarked path along the edge of three fields and down the middle of another to go through a gateway. Continue down the next field to a gate in the right-hand corner onto a lane. Follow it LEFT. (For **Walk B** turn right and follow the lane down to join your outward route.)

2 After a gate, by the nearby signposted Brenig and Hiraethog Trails bend LEFT up the stony track to a stile/gate by a barn. Go past the old farm and along a tree-lined green track to another stile/gate. Continue up to another stile ahead, then go up a sunken green track to a stile. Follow a path through the forest to a road. Follow it RIGHT, then at an information board on Pincyn Llys, turn LEFT and follow the signposted path through the trees, over a forestry track, and up to the Bagot monument on Pincyn Llys. Follow the waymarked Hiraethog/Brenig Way path west from the monument on a long gentle descent to a forestry track.

3 At the nearby junction turn RIGHT with the signposted Brenig Way along the track to rejoin the road. Follow it westwards past Cefn Du for about ¾ mile to a T- junction. Turn RIGHT. At crossroads by a house, continue up the road ahead Later when the road ends at a track leading down to a farm, continue ahead along the stony forestry track. At the end of a large turning area take a signposted path on the right along a green track to a stile/gate and on across a large field to a stile/boundary gate, then down to a gate near a ruin. Continue along the enclosed track to Cae Gwyn. Follow its access lane, then road down to Cyffylliog.

WALK 4

PINCYN LLYS FROM CLOCAENOG

DESCRIPTION A 6½ mile (**A**) or 5¾ mile (**B**) walk along open valleys and through forest to the monument on top of Pincyn Llys (See Walk 3), on part of the Hiraethog Trail (HT) and Brenig Way (BW). Allow about 3¼ hours.
START Clocaenog [SJ 084542].
DIRECTIONS Clocaenog is signposted from the B5105 Cerrigydrudion–Ruthin road. Park near the junction opposite the school.

I Go along the road opposite the school. When it bends right by the former

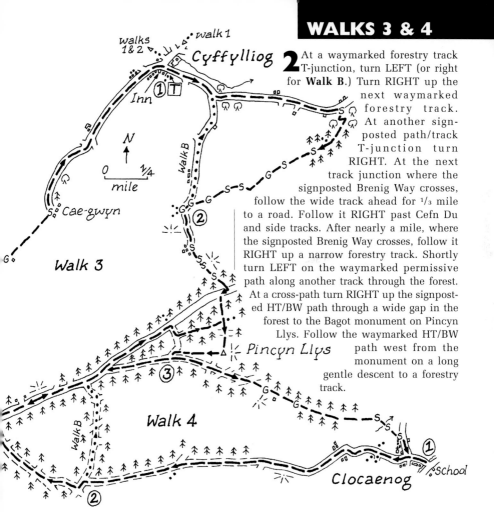

2 At a waymarked forestry track T-junction, turn LEFT (or right for **Walk B**.) Turn RIGHT up the next waymarked forestry track. At another signposted path/track T-junction turn RIGHT. At the next track junction where the signposted Brenig Way crosses, follow the wide track ahead for 1/3 mile to a road. Follow it RIGHT past Cefn Du and side tracks. After nearly a mile, where the signposted Brenig Way crosses, follow it RIGHT up a narrow forestry track. Shortly turn LEFT on the waymarked permissive path along another track through the forest. At a cross-path turn RIGHT up the signposted HT/BW path through a wide gap in the forest to the Bagot monument on Pincyn Llys. Follow the waymarked HT/BW path west from the monument on a long gentle descent to a forestry track.

National School – *built by Lord Bagot and once catering for 60 children daily and 45 on Sundays* – go up the narrow road ahead to St Foddyd's church. *Dating from 1538 and restored in the 19thC, it contains a fine 16thC rood screen, a 15thC font, and a bell, dating from 1638.* Continue up the road, later passing a large farm. Eventually, when the road bends left to a cattle grid, continue up the narrow track ahead and on along the forest edge. When it meets a wide stony forestry track keep ahead. *Near here was found a 5th/6th pillar-stone inscribed to 'Similinus Tovisacus', now in the National Museum of Wales. Such stones, set up to commemorate the dead, are the earliest evidence of Christianity.*

3 At the nearby track junction turn LEFT and follow the HT along the stony track, shortly descending past side tracks, then take the track's right fork down to another track. Follow it across an open area, then take the signposted HT path on the right down a narrow green track to a cottage. Follow its access track on a long steady descent into the valley, then take the signposted HT over a stile on the right. Go down the field and on to cross a stream and a stile beyond. Go across the next field to a stile in the corner onto a road. Follow it through Clocaenog to the start.

WALK 5
CWM ALWEN

DESCRIPTION A 7 mile walk (**A**) exploring the attractive wooded Alwen river valley and its adjoining low hills, lying between the small communities of Llanfihangel Glyn Myfyr and Pentre-llyn Cymmer, featuring an ancient church, an old drovers inn, an Iron-Age fort and good views. Allow about 3½ hours. The route includes a shorter 4½ mile walk (**B**).

START Llanfihangel Glyn Myfyr [SH 987496].

DIRECTIONS From Cerrigydrudion, take the B5105 towards Ruthin, and after descending the steep hill into Llanfihangel, turn left along a road just before the bridge and the Crown Inn. Follow it past the church to riverside picnic parking areas.

*L*lanfihangel Glyn Myfyr *was the birth-place of Owain Myfyr (Owen Jones) in 1741, a successful London businessman with an interest in old Welsh manuscripts. He was an important patron of Welsh literary works, including the publication of the 'Myfyrian Archaiology of Wales'. The poet William Wordsworth stayed here in 1824 and was inspired to write a poem about the area.*

Walk back along the road near the river, soon passing 13thC St Michael's church – *which was flooded to a height of 9 feet in 1781* – to reach the B5105. Turn LEFT across the splendid late 18thC single arched stone bridge over the Afon Alwen and past the Crown Inn – *an old drovers inn.* Continue up the right hand side of the road and just before the second bend, cross a stile on the left. Follow the signposted path up through trees above a stream, then the edge of a large field to a stile. *Pause to look back at the extensive views your short climb has achieved.* Cross a stony track and keep ahead across tussocky ground to the left of the stream to a waymark post at the small plantation corner. Follow the waymarked path past a small lake, then a reedy area beneath a small rocky ridge, and past a small pool to a stile in the fence ahead. Go across the field to go through a gate and another ahead on the right. Go along the field edge past the

paddock beneath Foel farm, angling away to a stile. Go across the next field to a stile, then turn LEFT up a road.

2 After passing between two large stone buildings, bend right with the road a few yards towards Bryn-y-gwrgi, then take a path up on the left leading back to a stile by the roof of the left building. Go half-LEFT to join a fence which you follow along a long field – *with superb views from the Berwyns in the south to Arenig Fawr in the west* – to a gate onto a stony forestry track. Follow it LEFT then northwards along the forest edge on the eastern side of Cwm Alwen – *enjoying panoramic views.* The track then continues through the forest on a long steady descent to a side track and up to a nearby crossroad of tracks. Here, turn LEFT and follow the track to a road by Hen Ysgubor/Tal y Cefn. Follow it LEFT down to a bridge over the Afon Alwen. (For **Walk B** return 15 yards to the Clocaenog Forest board, then angle right along a green track past a barrier gate. Follow it along the forest edge parallel with the river below to a gate at its end, and continue near the river. After a stile, go through the trees to cross the river by a delightful old footbridge to the road. Follow it left back to the start.)

3 Continue up the road, then turn RIGHT along the no through road to Caer Ddunod. Go past the house and continue down the road to the old farm standing beneath the ramparts of Caer Ddunod Iron-Age fort. Here bend LEFT on a waymarked path through gates between outbuildings and on between walls to a gate. Go along the edge of the reedy field beneath the fort then angle LEFT to a waymark post/telegraph pole above the Afon Alwen. Descend to the river then continue beside it beneath the wooded slope to a stile. Continue along an open stretch of river, soon passing a house opposite. About 100 yards further, angle away from the river up and across open pasture to eventually go through a waymarked gate at the end of a wall beyond a bend of the river. Go across the field to a prominent stile, then go slightly LEFT across open pasture to a point overlooking an Outdoor Education Centre in the scattered community of Pentre-

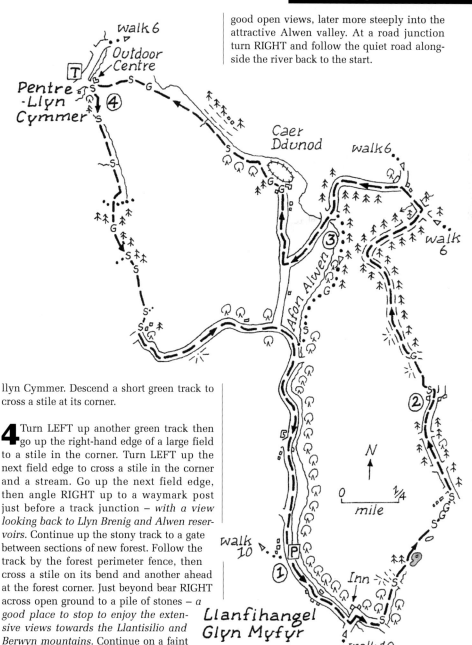

good open views, later more steeply into the attractive Alwen valley. At a road junction turn RIGHT and follow the quiet road alongside the river back to the start.

llyn Cymmer. Descend a short green track to cross a stile at its corner.

4 Turn LEFT up another green track then go up the right-hand edge of a large field to a stile in the corner. Turn LEFT up the next field edge to cross a stile in the corner and a stream. Go up the next field edge, then angle RIGHT up to a waymark post just before a track junction – *with a view looking back to Llyn Brenig and Alwen reservoirs.* Continue up the stony track to a gate between sections of new forest. Follow the track by the forest perimeter fence, then cross a stile on its bend and another ahead at the forest corner. Just beyond bear RIGHT across open ground to a pile of stones – *a good place to stop to enjoy the extensive views towards the Llantisilio and Berwyn mountains.* Continue on a faint sunken path towards a cottage to a stile/gate in the corner. Follow the green track ahead to a stile/gate and a road beyond. Continue down the delightful country road, enjoying

WALK 6
CRAIG BRON-BANOG

Pentre -Llyn Cymmer

DESCRIPTION An 8 mile figure of eight walk (**A**) exploring the afforested undulating countryside south east of Llyn Brenig, on paths, forestry tracks and quiet lanes. The route meanders through Clocaenog forest, passing a hidden waterfall and ancient standing stone, to its highest point – Craig Bron-Banog at 1640 feet/500 metres – offering panoramic views. It finishes with a delightful walk along a section of the Alwen river valley, passing by an Iron-Age hillfort. Allow about 4 hours. It can easily be shortened to a 6 mile walk (**B**) or 3¼ mile walk (**C**).
START Pentre-Llyn Cymmer [SH 974527]
DIRECTIONS Pentre-Llyn Cymmer, a small scattered farming community, lies just off the Cerrigydrudion- Llyn Brenig B4501 road. Go through the village, past a chapel and the Outdoor Education Centre. A few hundred yards further is a small roadside parking area on the right opposite a farm.

I Continue along the road, over the river Alwen and on past Forest Lodge. After the road bends left past Hendre, take a signposted path on the right up across the cleared forest to a forestry track by Cefn y Gors cottage. Take the signposted path opposite through conifers, soon crossing an old wall and later descending to a stony forestry track. Follow it RIGHT, soon skirting upland pasture. As the track begins to bend left, turn RIGHT along a narrower track. After 1/4 mile just after it bends right take an initially old walled path on the left down through the trees to cross a delightful small stone bridge over a river. Follow the sunken stony path up to a stony forestry track. Turn RIGHT. Down to your right is one of the highlights of the walk – *a beautiful stepped waterfall set amongst the conifers in a deep side valley.* If the river is in spate, this makes a wonderful sight. Now take the LEFT fork of the track up to reach the bend of a road at a prominent viewpoint.

2 Continue ahead along the road, soon descending to Hen Ysgubor and Tal y Cefn Isaf. (For **Walk C** continue down the road with the returning main route) Here, turn LEFT down a track. At a crossroad of forestry tracks turn RIGHT down the track. It later rises, then runs along the forest edge on the eastern edge of Cwm Alwen – *offering panoramic views* – before bending left to a road. Follow it ahead – *now on a waymarked section of the Hiraethog Trail* – later passing wall-enclosed upland pasture and a hill farm. The road then becomes enclosed by forest. (About 250 yards later, at a Hiraethog Trail waymark post, for **Walk B** turn sharp left up a forestry track through the forest to rejoin the returning main route at a track junction at point 4.) Continue along the road past a stony track on the left, then a track on the right, after which the road rises more steeply. Shortly after the road levels out, at a Hiraethog Trail finger post turn LEFT past the old standing stone of Maen Cred – *discovered and re-erected by the Forestry Commission in June 1991* – onto a nearby wide stony forestry track. *(½ mile to the east is an Iron-Age village.)* Follow it LEFT up through the forest and when it splits, keep straight ahead up to a crossroad of tracks by a Hiraethog Trail finger post.

3 Continue up the narrow stony track ahead, and at another finger post, bend RIGHT with the track up onto the open heather-covered top of Craig Bron – *Banog with its transmitter mast and experimen-*

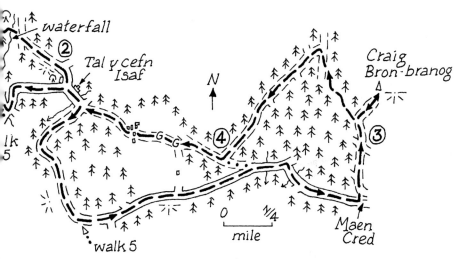

tal equipment designed to evaluate the effects of climate change on moorland. Do not enter the research area, but enjoy the stunning views: east over Clocaenog Forest to the Clwydian Range; south east to the Llantisilio Mountains; south west and west to the mountains of Snowdonia; north over Mynydd Hiraethog. Return down the track to the finger post on the bend. Turn RIGHT and follow the signposted path along an old narrow green track through the trees to a stony forestry track. Continue ahead towards distant wind turbines, then at the next track junction, turn LEFT. Follow the stony track down past a tall transmitter mast and side tracks to a forestry track T-junction. Turn RIGHT.

4 Follow the track to a crossroad of forestry tracks and turn LEFT along the narrow track to the forest edge. Follow the stony access track ahead down to Tai'n y Waen, passing through the farm and continuing along its access track to rejoin your outward route at a familiar crossroads of tracks. Continue ahead to the road by Tal y Cefn Isaf. Turn LEFT and follow the road down into the valley. Just before a bridge over the river Alwen, take a signposted path along a stony

forestry track on the right. Follow it along the attractive Alwen valley by the edge of the forest, passing the Iron-Age fort of Caer Ddunod visible on the opposite bank of the river, then Ddol uchaf to eventually join your outward route at a road.

Maen Cred

WALK 7
LLYN BRENIG

DESCRIPTION A popular 9½ mile way-marked Trail around Llyn Brenig for walkers and cyclists, on surfaced paths, tracks and roads, offering ever-changing views of the lake. The Trail features a section of an ancient highway crossing Pont-y-Brenig, which has many tales to tell, the northern edge of Gors Maen Llwyd Nature Reserve, and Bronze Age ceremonial and burial sites. Allow about 4 hours. A 1½ mile Nature Trail and a 2½ mile Archaeological Trail (see Walk 8) can easily be incorporated in this walk.
START Llyn Brenig Visitor Centre [SH 968547].
DIRECTIONS Llyn Brenig lies just east of the B4501 Cerrigydrudion-Denbigh road, and is well signposted.

*L*lyn Brenig *was first proposed as part of a twin reservoir scheme at the end of the 19thC by the then Corporation of Birkenhead to supply water direct to the town, but only Alwen reservoir was built. When Llyn Brenig was finally constructed between 1973–1976, its purpose was to regulate the flow of the river Dee, providing water for homes and industries in NE Wales. It is 2¹/₃ miles long and 148 feet at its deepest point. It is the fourth largest lake in Wales. It lies over 1200 feet above sea-level, with a climate that is wetter (average rainfall of 52 inches) and 2-3 degrees colder than at the coast.*

The lake attracts many birds - including great crested grebe, cormorant, and heron, wintering mallard, teal and goldeneye and in Spring, willow warblers return. It contains brown and locally reared rainbow trout and is an important fly fishing lake. Windsurfing, sailing and canoeing are also popular.

The Visitor Centre, open all year round, contains an interesting exhibition, shop, cafe, and bike hire facility. Welsh Water manage 377 hectares of forest and woodland surrounding the lake.

From the Visitor Centre car park follow the road northwards past the sailing club, then along the open western side of the lake past picnic areas. When the exit road bends

sharp left follow the road ahead, meandering along the edge of the lake. Later, at a junction with forestry tracks the road bends right (NE). *You are now on the old road from Pentrefoelas to Denbigh, which was replaced in 1826 by the turnpike road, now the A543.* Follow the road down to Pont-y-Brenig by the Nature Trail board. *Pont-y-Brenig, where the old road crossed the river, was once described as the most isolated place in North Wales, when the crossing of this wild inhospitable moorland could be a daunting experience for travellers. During the 18thC a local man Foulke Owen passed over this bridge during winter on his return from Denbigh, but never reached home. His body was found some weeks later buried in snow about one mile to the west at the precise spot where his wife dreamt that he had gone to sleep! Heilyn, a local highwayman, reputedly hid under the bridge waiting to rob drovers and farmers on their way back from Denbigh market. Folklore also tells of a young man who met a mysterious stranger dressed in grey clothes with gold buttons here. The stranger smiled, jumped off the bridge and vanished into the bog. Each time the young man passed that way he found a small pile of money and valuables at the same spot!* Continue up the road.

2 At a road/forestry track crossroads the Trail continues up the old forestry track ahead, past the returning Nature Trail path at post 6, and through two gates. The narrow Trail rises, then runs close to the B5401. *Nearby once stood a cottage occupied in the 19thC by a reputed miser with a hoard of golden sovereigns, who had seven locks on his door. Legend tells that after heavy snow, he discovered the remains of his elderly neighbour half eaten by her cat!* Shortly you reach an information board on Gors Maen Llwyd at a track junction and small parking area. *Gors Maen Llwyd Nature Reserve has been managed by the North Wales Wildlife Trust since 1988. The Reserve, consisting of heather moorland and peat bog, is rich in plants and insects, and supports various birds - e.g. skylark, stonechat, and hen harrier. The moorland habitat is particularly important for the increasingly rare*

Red and Black Grouse, so please keep to the waymarked trail from April through to September to avoid disturbing them. After a short stony track the Trail narrows and descends beside the B5401 along the edge of Gors Maen Llwyd. It then passes beneath the road before continuing on a steady climb beside it to join a side road. Follow it south past the nearby ruin of Bwlch-du – *a late 18thC farmhouse* – down to a small car park by former toilets.

3 Go to information boards at the nearby gate/cattle-grid, marking the start of the Archaeological Trail. Follow the stony lakeside track past the Bronze Age Ring Cairn and nearby Boncyn Arian burial mound, then Hafotty Sion Llwyd – *once a home for shepherds or bailiffs*. Continue with the track southwards along the eastern side of Llyn Brenig, passing along the edge of moorland and upland pasture – *enjoying good views* – and through a forest. *Lookiong back, on the skyline to the north west of the lake, is the ruin of Gwylfa Hiraethog, the former shooting lodge of the first Viscount Devonport, a politician and first chairman of the Port of London Authority. It was built in 1913 to replace a wooden lodge, made in Norway and erected at 1,627 feet on the moors in the early 1890s. It was an impressive large stone building designed by Sir Edwin Cooper, a notable architect. It had commanding views and was a prominent landmark in a vast area of wild moorland, often referred to as the 'Haunted House', and featured in several films. It was used as a residence for family and guests, including Lloyd George, during the grouse-shooting season until 1925, when it was sold. The family travelled in a special railway coach from London to Denbigh, before continuing their journey by horse wagon.* Eventually the Trail crosses the dam, then returns beside the lake to the Visitor Centre.

Llyn Brenig

WALK 8
ON THE TRAIL OF OUR ANCESTORS

DESCRIPTION This 2½ mile walk follows a waymarked Archaeological Trail through undulating upland pasture adjoining Llyn Brenig on its north east side. It visits important Bronze Age ceremonial and burial sites, and other places of archaeological interest investigated between 1973–1975 during the construction of Llyn Brenig, and offers extensive views. The Trail crosses open reedy, occasionally wet ground, and is best undertaken in good weather. Allow about 2 hours.

START Archaeological trail car park, Llyn Brenig (NE) [SH 984574]

DIRECTIONS From Cerrigydrudion take the B4501 north past Llyn Brenig, then take the Nantglyn road. After 1½ miles, follow a rough road on the right down to a small car park by the lake and former toilets.

1 The Trail starts from information boards by a nearby gate/cattle-grid. Follow the stony lakeside track past the signposted Brenig Way/Archaeological Trail to the Ring Cairn (**A**). *It served as a ceremonial monument from about 1680 BC. Later it was used as a cremation burial site.* Visit nearby Boncyn Arian (**B**) – *a large Bronze Age burial mound covering a central grave used about 2000 BC. Nearby is the site of a Mesolithic camp dating from around 5000 BC once occupied by Stone Age hunters.* Return to the signposted Brenig Way (Cyffylliog) and cross the stile. Angle LEFT up open pasture past two waymark posts to a third by the site of the Hafotai Settlement (**C**). *Dating from the 16thC, several stone huts, probably thatched with heather and rushes, once occupied both sides of the stream. They served as summer dwellings for the people who brought their animals to graze on the moors.* (For a shorter walk follow the nearby stream down to the start.)

2 The Trail now heads south across reedy terrain below the forest, guided by way-mark posts – *offering views of Llyn Brenig and the Snowdonia mountains* – later descending to a gate at the forest corner. Cross a stream, and go up the reedy slope past a post to another. Turn RIGHT to an information board by the impressive stone Platform Cairn (**D**) at a prominent viewpoint. *Built around 2000 BC and occupying an earlier site occupied by Bronze Age man, the cairn contained two separate cremation burials – one the remains of an adult and child placed in an urn beneath a large stone.*

3 From a waymark post beyond the Cairn go half-LEFT down the slope to an information board overlooking the site of Hen Ddinbych (**E**) – a large medieval farmhouse. Descend the slope and pass the left side of the site to a waymark post. Continue towards wind turbines to join a path parallel with the nearby fence to a stile/gate in its corner. Continue with the Trail, guided by posts, shortly bending right across the heather cov-

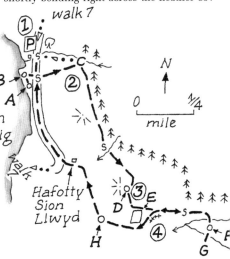

ered flat side valley, over a stream, and on to reach a Bronze Age kerb-cairn (**F**). *The wooden posts mark the post-holes of a possible prehistoric hut, over which the cairn containing a cremation burial was built. Nearby is Maen Cleddau (**G**) – a large glacial stone, reputed to have been broken by a giant's sword.* Retrace your steps to the fence corner before Hen Ddinbych.

4 Now bear LEFT on a path near the fence to pass round the southern end of Hen Ddinbych. After a further 100 yards leave the fence and head half-RIGHT up the slope to another Bronze Age kerb-cairn (**H**). Continue across upland pasture towards the northern end of the lake to a post, then descend a stony track leading to Hafotty Sion Llwyd. *Rebuilt in 1881 using some stone from Hen Ddinbych, this was the home of shepherds or bailiffs.* Follow the nearby lakeside track back to the start.

soon overlooking a narrow section of the lake. The track then bends away from the lake, later passing an area of cleared forest. The Trail then follows a stony path down through the trees, soon leaving the forest to rejoin the lake. The path follows the lake

WALK 9
ALWEN TRAIL

DESCRIPTION A 7 mile waymarked Trail for walkers and mountain bikers around Alwen Reservoir, built in the early 20thC to supply water to Birkenhead. The route follows surfaced paths and tracks through forest, along the lakeside edge and across open exposed moorland, reaching a height of 1410 feet/430 metres. It is best undertaken in good conditions. Allow about 4 hours.
START Car park, the dam, Alwen Reservoir [SH 956530].
DIRECTIONS The Alwen Reservoir, also Hafod-y-Llanganol, is signposted off the B4501, midway up a hill. Follow the stony track, soon taking its left fork. After passing between houses, turn left to park by the impressive dam, whose first stone was laid in October 1911.

1 Return to the bend of the track and take the signposted path to Pen-y-Ffrith past a gate ahead. The Trail goes along a stony track, then passes through iron railings and continues as a stony path through trees up to join a wide forestry track. Follow it past a large stone building and up to where it splits into three. Keep with the waymarked right fork, then at a track junction, bear LEFT,

edge, then bends inland to cross a stream, and continues through an area of forest, leaving it by a kissing gate. Just beyond, follow the waymarked Trail LEFT to join a stony track which descends to a long footbridge over the reservoir.

2 After crossing the footbridge the path continues to old sheepfolds, crosses a stream, then rises steadily across open moorland. Shortly after a kissing gate, you reach the Trail's highest point, offering panoramic views. The path now steadily descends to gates/stile and down to a forestry track above a stream. The Trail continues through trees, then follows a forestry track. Later it angles off the track down towards the lake, bends to cross a stream in a side valley and rises through trees to join another forestry track, parallel with the lake. Just after it bends right the Trail turns left down through trees towards the lake and continues near the lakeside to cross the dam.

WALK 10

CAER CARADOG

DESCRIPTION A 6 mile walk (**A**) exploring a little visited area of interesting attractive countryside, with extensive views. The route heads west from Cwm Alwen and visits a small hidden attractive reservoir. Later it rises, initially on an old green track, across upland pasture to pass the remains of Caer Caradog, an Iron-Age hillfort. It then follows the waymarked Hiraethog Trail, first along a delightful old drovers' road across upland pasture beneath Mwdwl-eithin, then down to Llanfihangel, with its old drovers' inn and ancient church to visit. Allow about 3½ hours. An alternative 3¼ mile walk (**B**) is included. For information on Llanfihangel Glyn Myfyr see Walk 5.
START Llanfihangel Glyn Myfyr [SH 987496] See Walk 5.

I From the furthest picnic area by an adventure play area just before the former school take a signposted path through a gate on the left. Follow a rising stony track above a stream. After a gate take the main track bearing RIGHT to go through a gate over the stream. Go half-LEFT up the field to rejoin the track and follow it to gates, past a stone barn to another gate. Continue up the green track past the old farmhouse. As it bends left across the stream continue ahead briefly along its left-hand bank, then up the field edge by an old reedy sunken track to a gap in its corner. Follow the green track ahead for 10 yards, and go through a gap in the left in the gorse-covered boundary. Continue along the right-hand field edge by the old reedy track towards a wind turbine, then in the corner bend LEFT up to a waymarked gate in the top corner. Go through a gap in the old wall just ahead, and follow the boundary on your left up to go through a waymarked gate in it, near the corner. (For **Walk B**, just above turn left and follow a wide track, then a lane, to the B5105. Take the signposted bridleway through a gate opposite. Angle right away from the stony track up the field towards a wind turbine past a telegraph pole to a waymarked double gate adjoining the track. Go along another green track to a waymarked gate, then up the slope, passing to the right of another turbine, and across the field to a waymarked gate. Angle LEFT down to a waymarked gate below, then down to another gate by the farm. Go along its access track to a road. Follow it left down to Llanfihangel.)

2 For **Walk A** go through the waymarked gate just above. Head west (waymark misleading) across upland pasture to a waymarked gate just before ruined buildings by a rocky escarpment. Go past the old outbuilding and through a gate on the right just beyond the ruined cottage. Angle LEFT to the boundary and go down the field edge to see the hidden small attractive rowan tree edged part lily-covered reservoir – *home for wildfowl and a quiet spot for fishing*. Retrace your steps, and after passing through the gate by the cottage, go half-RIGHT and through a waymarked gate. Go half-LEFT to another waymarked gate. Turn RIGHT along the next field edge to a gate by a nearby house and down its access track to a gate. Turn LEFT along a lane past Maes Tyddyn farm, and on to reach the B5105. Turn RIGHT down the grass verge.

3 Shortly, take a signposted path through the farmyard of Tyn y Mynydd opposite to cross a stream and a stile beyond. Follow an old green track up to a gate, then up across the open western slopes of Y Drum – *offering excellent views west towards Cerrigydrudion and the mountains of Snowdonia beyond*. After passing a short section of collapsed wall, go through a gate ahead. Continue up by the fence to a gate in its corner at its highest point. Continue beside the fence, with the distinctive ramparts of Caer Caradog hillfort to your right. *The Iron-Age fort, situated at about 1246 feet/380 metres on a strategic site overlooking important valley routes, has a circular rampart of earth and shale enclosing an area of about 2 acres. It is reputed to be the legendary fortified base of King Caractacus, who was captured by the Romans and taken in chains to Rome.* The fence descends to a gate. Go past the fence corner ahead and down the field to a ladder-stile onto a minor road. Follow it LEFT and at a junction, keep

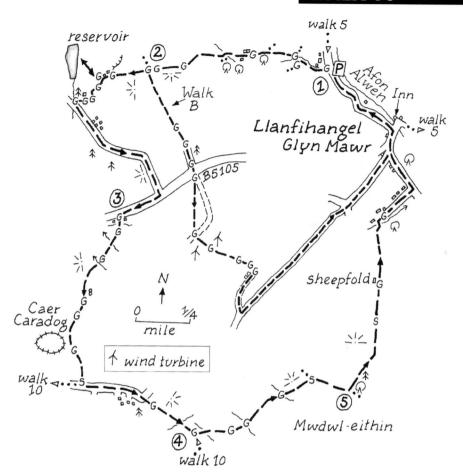

ahead to pass two farms. When the road bends left, go along a green track ahead to a gate. Continue along this delightful enclosed old drovers route to a gate into open country, where you join the Hiraethog Trail.

4 Continue with the green track near the wall rising steadily up the hillside, passing through two gates. After another it continues along the edge of upland pasture and the heather-covered slopes of Mwdwl-eithin to a stile/gate. Continue along the green track – *enjoying the extensive views.*

5 Just before the next gate on the track, the waymarked Hiraethog Trail bends LEFT and follows another green track on a long

steady descent towards Llanfihangel, to a ladder-stile/gate, then a gate by a sheepfold. Now follow an old gorse lined green track down the hillside to a gate. Go ahead down the next field edge to join a stony track, which bends down towards a farm. Cross the nearby footbridge over the stream to a small gate beneath the barn. Go through the gate ahead and along the old farm's driveway. At a junction, turn LEFT along the road into Llanfihangel. At the next junction, turn RIGHT to reach the B5105. Cross the road and follow it down to the junction. If not tempted by the nearby Crown Inn – *a traditional pub with a scenic beer garden above the river* – turn LEFT along the road past 13thC St Michael's church back to the start.

17

WALK II

CWM CEIRW

DESCRIPTION A 8½ mile walk exploring the remote hills and valleys lying between the ancient communities of Llangwm and Cerrigydrudion, incorporating sections of the Hiraethog Trail at both ends, offering extensive views. The route rises from Llangwm to upland pasture above the Ceirw valley at 1148 feet/350 metres, then follows an old drovers' route past an Iron-Age hillfort down to Cerrigydrudion. It returns past prominent hillside wind turbines at 1378 feet/420 mete and an impressive 14thC house. Allow about 5 hours.

START Llangwm [SH 966446] or alternatively Cerrigydrudion [SH 954488].

DIRECTIONS Llangwm is signposted from the A5. Park by the former village church. See Walk 12 for the alternative start and join the route at the A5 (point 4).

L langwm is reputed to be the site of a 10thC battle when the Prince of South Wales was slain by the Prince of North Wales. Traditionally an agricultural community, where cattle/sheep were fattened before drovers moved them to London markets it was noted for its large black cattle fair held in April and once produced knitted stockings sold in London and Liverpool markets.

I Follow the road back through the village, over the river and past The Lodge, where it bends right. Shortly take the signposted Hiraethog Trail path on the left up through a wood to a small gate. Go half-LEFT up the field, over a track, and on to a stile in the first corner. Descend to another stile by a farm, then turn LEFT through a gate at a barn below. Go through the farmyard and a gate on the right, then follow the farm's access track down past a chapel to a road. Turn LEFT then cross a stile on the right. Go through a kissing gate opposite and another below, then follow the river Ceirw along the field to cross a large footbridge over it. Go along the field edge to a kissing gate onto the A5. Turn LEFT, then follow the signposted path through the farm opposite to a gate at the right side of the house. Follow a track behind

outbuildings to another, which meanders steadily up the hillside. At its end follow the hedge up the field to cross a stile in it after about 100 yards. Follow the fence along the top of the field to a gate at its end by a farm.

2 Follow a stony track to another gate ahead and past a wood to a track T-junction. Turn RIGHT along the track to a stile/gate and up to another stile/gate. Continue along the track, shortly bending up to go through a waymarked gate. Follow the wall on your left to another gate in the field corner, then on to a stile/gate. Beyond bear LEFT with the wall down to a finger post by a track. Here you leave the Hiraethog Trail by turning LEFT through the nearby gate and following a delightful enclosed old drovers' track to a road. Follow it ahead past two farms.

3 At a junction keep ahead, shortly passing Caer Caradog Iron-Age fort, with its gorse-covered ramparts, up to your right. (See Walk 7). The scenic upland road – *an old drovers' route* – then steadily descends towards Cerrigydrudion. At Felin Bwlch turn LEFT on a signposted path along a stony track leading to Fron Deg. The track bends between the house and an outbuilding into a small caravan site. Just after it bends left turn RIGHT between caravans to a kissing gate. Follow the kissing-gated path along the edge of two fields, past outbuildings, and down a stony track to the road in Cerrigydrudion. Follow the short path opposite to the A5. Cross the road with care and follow the pavement past a nearby cafe and The Saracens Head. *Note the old milestone. Holyhead, Corwen – but where is Cernioge? See Walk 14 for the answer.*

4 Turn LEFT down Ty'n-y-Rhyd and follow the road over the river and up to a junction. Turn LEFT past Pen-y-Bryn Bach, then follow the road into open country. Just after passing Tai'n y Rhos / Creigiau take a signposted path over a stile on the right. Go across the field and down to a stile, then along the next field edge to a ruined cottage. Turn LEFT down to a gate, and on across the next field to cross a footbridge over the

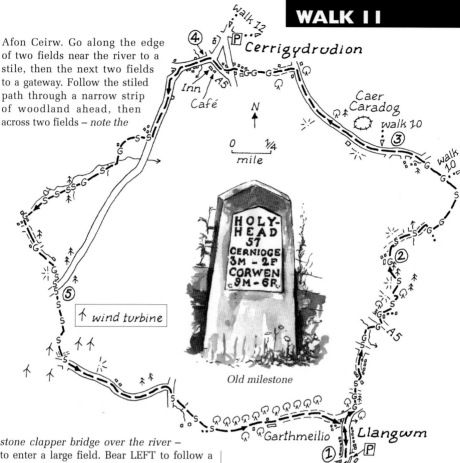

Afon Ceirw. Go along the edge of two fields near the river to a stile, then the next two fields to a gateway. Follow the stiled path through a narrow strip of woodland ahead, then across two fields – *note the*

Cerrigydrudion

Caer Caradog
walk 10

Old milestone

wind turbine

stone clapper bridge over the river –
to enter a large field. Bear LEFT to follow a stream towards the left side of a large farm to a gate by an outbuilding onto a stony track beyond. Turn LEFT, then go up the farm's concrete driveway. On its bend by a building go through the middle of three gates. Go up the right bank of the nearby reedy stream and on up to an old embanked boundary/fence. Bear RIGHT up the boundary – *enjoy-ing extensive views into Cwm Penanner –* to a gate in the fence into the adjoining field. Follow the fence to cross a stile near the field corner and another ahead onto the road.

5 Cross the stile opposite to join the Hiraethog Trail back to Llangwm. Follow the waymarked stiled path up two fields towards wind turbines, then go half-RIGHT across a tussocky/reedy area and up onto a small grass shelf. Bear RIGHT round to cross

a stile then follow the fence past the large turbine and a gate across its access track to a stile onto a road. Follow it LEFT down past a farm to the B4501. Turn RIGHT down it, then take the signposted Trail over a stile opposite. Follow the fence down the large field edge, over a stream and on to a stile in the corner. Briefly keep ahead, then angle down the slope to a stile in the bottom corner onto a stony track. Follow it beneath a bluebell wood to Gamekeepers Cottage, then a concrete road through mature wood-land to Garthmeilio – *a 14thC estate house.* Continue along its driveway. Later, as it bends left towards the road, keep ahead past a ruin, then follow a nearby cottage's access track to the road at Llangwm.

CRAIG YR IYRCHEN

DESCRIPTION A 6½ mile walk (**A**) exploring attractive upland pasture and moorland fringes north of Cerrigydrudion, rising in stages to a height of 1476 feet/450 metres with excellent views. The route crosses lower pastures, then rises very steadily up a quiet lane, before following a waymarked path across the upper slopes of Craig yr Iyrchen. It then descends to the ancient hamlet of Cefn Brith, before returning by road and field paths to Cerrigydrudion, where the Coffee Shop makes a good ending to the walk. Allow about 3½ hours. The route also offers a simple 1¼ mile walk (**B**).
START Cerrigydrudion [SH 954488]
DIRECTIONS Cerrigydrudion lies just off the A5. There is a signposted car park beside a former garage at the beginning of Ruthin Road (B5105).

*C*errigydrudion *is the largest settlement in Mynydd Hiraethog. Its name meaning 'the stones of the daring ones' is reputedly a reference to a large pile of stones once located near the church. Local tradition says that they were the prison in which Cyn-vrig Rwth, a lawless chieftain, kept his captives. The original 18thC London-Holyhead turnpike coach road once passed through the village centre, but in the early 19thC, Thomas Telford diverted the route, building a new road from Cerrigydrudion to Glasfryn, now the A5. Much of the surrounding grazing land was let to Anglesey dealers for fattening up their cattle on the way to the Midland markets. The village was an important shoeing station and one of its famous sons was the 17thC drover and poet, Edward Morus – still droving at 82! In the 19thC villagers were involved in cattle/sheep breeding, spinning of woollen yarn and knitting of stockings. There used to be five fairs a year. In 1854, George Borrows, the eminent traveller and writer of 'Wild Wales' stayed at 'the Lion - whether the white, black, red or green Lion I do not know' after walking 20 miles from Llangollen on his way to Bangor. Here he enjoyed good conversation with a doctor and a Welsh-speaking Italian. In the centre stand St Mary Magdalene's church, dating from the16thC and restored in 1874, and alms-houses built in 1716.*

Walk east along the pavement through Cerrigydrudion to reach the driveway to Bwlch y beudy at the village outskirts. On the skyline beyond the white cottage ahead are the distinctive ramparts of Caer Caradog Iron-Age hillfort. Turn up the driveway, then take a signposted path over a ladder-stile on the left. Follow the stiled path along the edge of four fields – *enjoying good views over Cerrigydrudion, and on a clear day to the mountains of Snowdonia* – to reach the B4501. Go along the road opposite towards Cefn Brith past Gwynfa and a stile on the left about 30 yards beyond (the short/return route). Continue along the road. After passing a stream and a driveway on the right the road rises gently.

2 At a junction, turn RIGHT and go up the minor road. After a while it levels out to provide panoramic views west along the wide valley towards the mountains of Snowdonia. This delightful walled road continues up the hillside, past a side road and a house. At the next junction keep ahead to pass beneath Parc Newydd. After a gate the more open lane rises gently across upland pasture grazed by sheep – *soon with views east to wind turbines above Clocaenog Forest, and ahead to the forest hiding Alwen reservoir, later glimpsing the dam tower among the trees.*

3 Eventually you reach Craig-yr-iyrchen-fawr. Here take the signposted Hiraethog Trail over a stile on the left. Go up the old sunken path, soon becoming a more distinct old track and rising steadily into open country. Just visible on the skyline to the north-east is the ruin of Gwylfa Hiraethog – *the former shooting lodge of Viscount Devonport (For details see Walk 7).* After a small quarry, the waymarked path rises half-LEFT, passing above another small quarry, then continues up to a stile in a fence. Now angle LEFT to follow a meandering sketchy path

onto the small rise ahead. Looking back is a glimpse of Alwen Reservoir. Continue west across the tussocky/heather covered terrain for about 75 yards to a waymark post at a prominent viewpoint on Craig yr Lyrchen. *Enjoy the views east to Clocaenog Forest; south east to the Llantisilio Mountains; south to the Berwyn Range ; and south west to the Aran and Arenig mountains.* Continue along a narrow green track – *with new views of Llyn y Cwrt and on a clear day the mountains of Snowdonia –* shortly steadily descending past a waymark post. When it bends left go to a nearby waymark post by another rising green track. Follow the waymarked narrow path ahead through an area of bracken and gorse, over a cross-track, then through heather to cross a ladder-stile onto a track – *a good place for a break to enjoy the extensive views. Snowdon, Moel Siabod, the Glyders, Tryfan and the Carneddau range dominate the skyline on a clear day.*

4 Turn LEFT along the track, soon steadily descending the hillside. After a gate continue down a walled lane. At a crossroad, in the hamlet of Cefn Brith, turn LEFT, and at the next junction, continue ahead. Follow the quiet country road back towards Cerrigydrudion for about 1½ miles, later joining your outward route. *This was the original 18thC turnpike road.* Just before Gwynfa, take the signposted path over the stile on the right. Walk beside the wall to cross another stile in the corner. Turn LEFT beside the wall down the next field edge to go through

a gateway in the corner. Turn RIGHT and follow the wall down the field, then after about 75 yards go half-LEFT to cross a stile and a stream in a wet reedy area. Go through reeds and up the field edge to a kissing gate/gate in the corner onto the road opposite the school. Turn RIGHT to reach the centre of Cerrigydrudion and the nearby Coffee Shop.

WALK 13
CWM PENANNER

DESCRIPTION This 6½ mile walk (**A**) explores a little-known upland area and the hidden attractive valley of Cwm Penanner with its scattered farming community. The route, which uses quiet attractive country roads, field paths and a delightful open upland bridleway, offers a great sense of space and excellent ever changing distant views. Allow about 3½ hours. It can easily be shortened to a 3¾ mile walk (**B**) or varied using the link paths/roads shown.

START Crossroads above Cwm Penanner [SH 918480].

DIRECTIONS From Glasfryn, take the minor road heading south off the A5, opposite a pottery. Follow it past a side road to rise steadily up the hillside to its highest point and on down to the signposted Bala, Cerrigydrudion, Blaen Cwm, Glasfryn crossroads, where there is a small off-road parking area.

Walk back along the road towards Glasfryn, and after nearly ⅓ mile, take a signposted path through a gate on the right. Keep ahead to pass to the left of a ruined cottage (The Lodge), over a stream and on to cross a stile. Now follow a stiled path along the edge of several fields – *said to have been regularly walked by an elderly lady, the last occupant of the cottage, on her way to church in Cerrigydrudion* – to a road. Continue ahead along the road. Shortly take a signposted path through a gate on the right opposite a small ruin. Ignore the track leading to a transmitter mast, but go half-RIGHT up the field – *with a good view across to Snowdon, the Glyders and Carneddau mountains* – and on to the wall/ fence corner by two telegraph poles – *offering your first view into the hidden Cwm Penanner, with wind-turbines on the high ridge, and the Llangwm hills beyond.* Go past the gate and through a gap in the fence into the next field. When the fence on your left joins a wall just ahead, angle gently away from the boundary to a stile/gate by a sheepfold. Go round the left hand edge of a large reedy area and on to a gate onto a nearby farm's access lane.

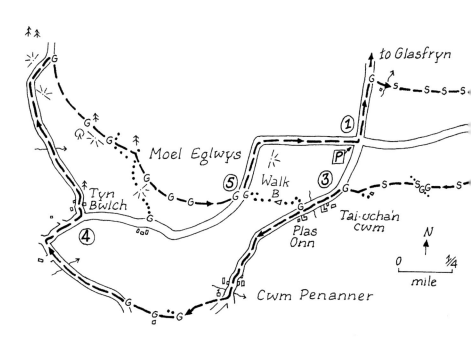

2 Cross the stile opposite, then go half-LEFT to join the fence on your left above the farm. At its corner, continue ahead across the slope beneath rock outcrops, and down to a small gate in the fence corner. Go to a stone stile ahead then along the next field by the wall to stile in the corner. Follow the boundary on your left along the large field past two gates then go through the third gate in the recessed field corner at a barbed wire fence into the adjoining field. Turn RIGHT down to a gate across a track. Go up the track through gorse for about 10 yards then angle LEFT through a gap to a hidden stile in the nearby fence. Now go half-RIGHT across the large field, soon descending to a stile in the fence ahead, about 75 yards above a ruin. Just beyond angle LEFT down across rough pasture to join a track, which you follow to a road. Turn LEFT.

3 Follow the road past Tai-ucha'n-cwm – *note the Lion 1720 datestone on the front of the house* – and on past Plas Onn. (For **Walk B**, go through a gate opposite the gable end of the house and follow a green track that winds its way up the hillside to a higher road at point 5.) Follow the road down into Cwm Penanner to the old Ty Mawr chapel and attached chapel house by the river and a road junction. A signpost indicates that you are only 7 miles from Bala! *The Methodist chapel, dating from 1828, then rebuilt in 1898, has been an important focal point for this scattered community.* Continue along the road and at the corner of the churchyard, follow the signpost-ed path beside the boundary on your right across reedy terrain. Later the path angles away from the boundary to go through a way-marked gate. Follow the boundary on your right, and at its first corner, follow an inter-mittent stone-paved path part hidden in the reeds to a gate by a cottage. Continue ahead along the left-hand edge of a large reedy area, by an old field boundary. When it bends right, keep ahead across the field to a small gate in the boundary ahead to rejoin the road. Follow it up to a junction. Turn RIGHT and follow the road up to another junction.

4 Turn LEFT up past Tyn Bwlch. Follow the road for about ¾ mile beneath the eastern slopes of Garn Prys. After a level section the road bends down towards the expansive valley – *with the mountains of Snowdonia visible to the north-west.* As the road becomes less steep, you reach two gates on the right. Here go through the higher gate and up a green track (a bridleway). It soon levels out and continues across upland pasture, passing through a gate, then between trees – *with excellent open views.* After another gate, keep ahead. When the track splits, continue ahead on the higher fork, soon crossing a cross-track and rising to a gate. The delightful scenic gated green track continues round the higher slopes of Moel Eglwys – *offering panoramic views as far as the Berwyns and Arans* – before descending gently to the road.

5 Follow this delightful high-level road contouring the eastern slopes of Moel Eglwys and upland pasture back to the start.

Chapel in Cwm Penanner

WALK 14

LLYN Y CWRT

DESCRIPTION A 6½ mile meandering walk (**A**) across the lower northern slopes of the wide Cwm Merddwr valley near Glasfryn, featuring a small attractive hidden upland lake, an old coaching inn, now a farm, delightful old walled tracks and extensive views. The route follows a section of the Hiraethog Trail across upland pasture, reaching a height of 1148 feet/350 metres, before descending to Cernioge. It then heads north past Llyn y Cwrt to join the outward route, later making a direct return. Allow about 3½ hours. The route offers two shorter walks of 4½ miles (**B**) and 2 miles (**C**).
START Glasfryn [SH 502917].
DIRECTIONS Glasfryn lies on the A5 midway between Pentrefoelas and Cerrigydrudion. Car parking in the village is time restricted, so park in a lay-by at the western end of the village.

1 Walk east along the A5 through the village, then take the side road signposted to Cefn Brith by the old school. After nearly ½ mile on a bend, cross a stile on the left to join the Hiraethog Trail. Angle up the field to join a wall on the left. Follow the wall past a joining fence, over a stream, and on to cross a stone stile in the field corner. Continue along the next field edge to a ladder-stile and through a gate beyond. Continue ahead along an old walled green track – *enjoying extensive views from the Berwyn Range to the mountains of Snowdonia* – to a gate. Go along the field by the wall to another gate into a small walled area containing two other gates.

2 Go through the gate ahead. (For **Walk C** then turn left. Go down the edge of two fields to a house, then follow its access track to the A5 by the garage.) Continue ahead along the field and down to pass through gates by sheepfolds and over a stream. Follow a track up the next field edge to a gate onto the bend of a stony track – *with a good view now of Llyn y Cwrt* – and follow it through a gate ahead. Continue ahead beside the wall along the reedy field edge, over a

stream and on up to a stile/old gate. Follow the wall up the next large field and on to a waymarked gate ahead. Go up and across the field to a waymark post. *On a clear day, Moel Siabod, Snowdon, the Glyders, Tryfan and the Carneddau range dominate the skyline ahead. To your right is the high moorland ridge of Mwdwl-eithin, and ahead are two wind turbines.* Continue along a small grassy ridge and down to a finger post, where a green track angles in from the left (your return route). Keep ahead on the waymarked trail, through a gap in the wall to a stile/gate beyond. Follow the wall to another finger post at a junction of paths.

3 Here you leave the Trail by turning LEFT through a small gate. Follow an old walled gated green track past a wind turbine down to an old hillfarm. Go between outbuildings and the house and down to go through a waymarked gate. Take the waymarked path leading LEFT across the top of the field to a gate in the corner. Go over a stream and up the middle of the large field to cross a stone stile by a gate in the wall ahead. Follow the wall on the left down the long field – *with a good view of Llyn y Cwrt fringed by alder woodland* – to a gate in the bottom corner. Continue to a gate across a track ahead and follow it up to join the nearby farm's access track. Follow it to a cattle-grid and down to go through a gate by sheepfolds just before the A5, with Cernioge Mawr opposite. (For **Walk B** simply walk along the pavement on the A5 for ½ mile back to the start.)

4 Turn LEFT to go through a waymarked gate, then LEFT up the field edge to a gate and continue to another gate at the wood corner. Go along the wood edge to reach Llyn y Cwrt with its stone boathouse. Continue along the lake edge, through a gate and on through another gate just beyond the lake corner. Go across two fields above the lake, then across the next field to the far boundary. Follow it up to the farm and go through a gate in the corner by the house. Turn LEFT along its access track between farm buildings, then go through a gate up on the right.

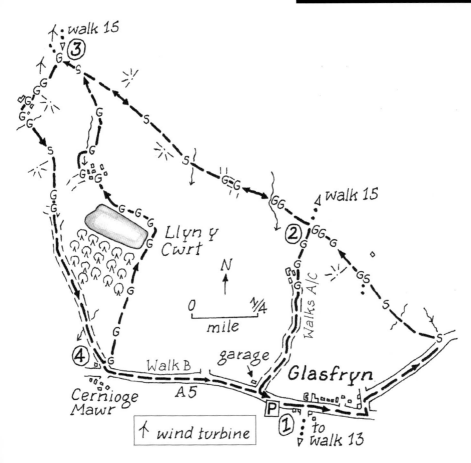

walk 15

③

Llyn y Cwrt

walk 15

②

Walks A/C

N

0 ¼ mile

④

Walk B

garage

Glasfryn

Cernioge Mawr

A5

P

①

to walk 13

⟨ wind turbine ⟩

Follow a stony track up to a gate, then above a shallow side valley to another gate and on to rejoin the Hiraethog Trail at the finger post passed earlier. Now follow your outward route back to small gated area at point 2.

Don't go through it but turn RIGHT down the edge of two fields to a house, then follow its access track to the A5 by the garage and the start.

Llyn y Cwrt

WALK 15

MWDWL-EITHIN

DESCRIPTION An exhilarating 8¼ mile walk (**A**) around the remote high moorland ridge of Mwdwl-eithin, lying between the A5 and the A543, or a 7¾ mile walk (**B**) to its summit (1755 feet/532 metres) for breathtaking all-round views. After a section of the Hiraethog Trail the route rises north to cross the eastern slopes of Mwdwl-eithin to join the Alwen Trail. Walk B heads up to Mwdwl-eithin's summit, with its cairns, trig point and shelter, then descends its western slope and follows an old track to rejoin the main route. Walk A descends to a side valley near the neck of the Alwen reservoir, then follows an ancient green road up to a bwlch, before descending across moorland and returning across upland pasture on the Hiraethog Trail. *This moorland romp, wet in places, is for experienced, well equipped hillwalkers only, and should be avoided in poor visibility.* Allow about 5 hours.

START Glasfryn [SH 502917] See Walk 14.

I Follow Follow the instructions in the first section of Walk 14.

2 Go through the gate on the right and up a gated walled track – *used by drovers to move cattle and sheep from upland pastures on their journey to distant markets* – to its end by sheepfolds, into open upland country. Continue along the near-side edge of a small grassy ridge, passing to the left of a reedy area. After about 100 yards, bear LEFT along a faint green track, soon a path, to ford a stream. Bear RIGHT to follow a clear path parallel with an old wall on your left. After crossing a stream, keep ahead on a faint green track, with the remains of the wall on your left, to go through a gate in a more substantial wall ahead.

3 Continue ahead to follow a path rising steadily up the heather covered southern slopes of Mwdwl-eithin towards two small trees on the horizon, later, passing to the right of the small hill on which they stand, then follow a path up a tussocky/reedy area, passing a small tree to your right.

Keep ahead along the edge of heather-covered high ground to your left, passing just to the right of another small tree. Shortly the path levels out – *with views to the summit cairns on Mwdwl-eithin and the mountains of Snowdonia.*

4 The path now skirts beneath the heather-covered high ground to your right, then crosses a more expansive area of heather – *with views now across to Alwen reservoir and its surrounding forest.* The intermittent path heads north, first contouring, then steadily descending across the bracken and heather covered eastern slopes of Mwdwl-eithin. It then crosses a level wet reedy area. After passing above a small ruin continue in the same direction across drier moorland to eventually join the stony Alwen Trail at its highest point and descend to a kissing gate below. (For **Walk B** turn left up a quad track through the heather with the fence on your right to the summit of Mwdwl-eithin. Cross the fence to the nearby large stone cairn, stone shelter, trig point and smaller cairn. Return to the fence. Don't cross it, but follow it down Mwdwl-eithin's heather-covered western slope to where it angles left at a junction with an older fence. Below you will see a clear narrow green track, used by ponies, heading through the expansive heather towards two wind turbines. First follow the old fence right to a nearby gate, then descend to a distinctive green area. Go to your right a few yards to find the now hidden old track. Follow it towards the turbines, later becoming a path. Ignore a path bending left towards the fence, but continue down upland pasture to a finger post by a wall near the lower turbine to join the main route at point 7.)

5 From the kissing gate follow the Trail down into a side valley. Immediately after crossing a stream, turn LEFT and go past sheepfolds to a tree by the small ruin of Nant Heilyn – *the former home of Heilyn, an 18thC highwayman, who used to rob drovers and farmers on their way home from Denbigh market. His hoard of stolen silver and gold may still lie hidden nearby! It makes a good stopping place.* Now follow

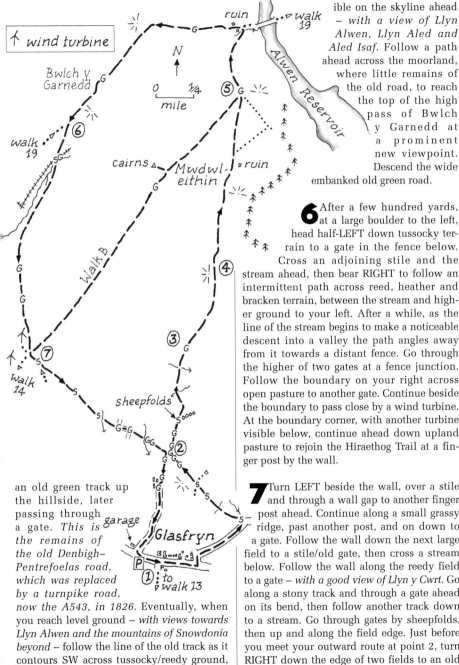

ible on the skyline ahead – *with a view of Llyn Alwen, Llyn Aled and Aled Isaf.* Follow a path ahead across the moorland, where little remains of the old road, to reach the top of the high pass of Bwlch y Garnedd at a prominent new viewpoint. Descend the wide embanked old green road.

6 After a few hundred yards, at a large boulder to the left, head half-LEFT down tussocky terrain to a gate in the fence below. Cross an adjoining stile and the stream ahead, then bear RIGHT to follow an intermittent path across reed, heather and bracken terrain, between the stream and higher ground to your left. After a while, as the line of the stream begins to make a noticeable descent into a valley the path angles away from it towards a distant fence. Go through the higher of two gates at a fence junction. Follow the boundary on your right across open pasture to another gate. Continue beside the boundary to pass close by a wind turbine. At the boundary corner, with another turbine visible below, continue ahead down upland pasture to rejoin the Hiraethog Trail at a finger post by the wall.

7 Turn LEFT beside the wall, over a stile and through a wall gap to another finger post ahead. Continue along a small grassy ridge, past another post, and on down to a gate. Follow the wall down the next large field to a stile/old gate, then cross a stream below. Follow the wall along the reedy field to a gate – *with a good view of Llyn y Cwrt.* Go along a stony track and through a gate ahead on its bend, then follow another track down to a stream. Go through gates by sheepfolds, then up and along the field edge. Just before you meet your outward route at point 2, turn RIGHT down the edge of two fields to an old farm, then follow its access track to the A5 by the garage near the start.

an old green track up the hillside, later passing through a gate. *This is the remains of the old Denbigh–Pentrefoelas road, which was replaced by a turnpike road, now the A543, in 1826.* Eventually, when you reach level ground – *with views towards Llyn Alwen and the mountains of Snowdonia beyond* – follow the line of the old track as it contours SW across tussocky/reedy ground, with the A543 below. Later keep to its left bank to eventually go through a gate vis-

WALK 16

CWM MERDDWR

DESCRIPTION A 5¾ mile walk **(A)** exploring the undulating countryside of the Merddwr valley near Pentrefoelas, The route features a delightful old drovers' road, a 18thC house, a 12thC motte, excellent views and an old coaching inn or café for refreshments at the end. Allow about 3 hours. A shorter 3¾ mile walk **(B)** is included.

START Car park, Pentrefoelas [SH 874 514]

DIRECTIONS In Pentrefoelas leave the A5 and take the road opposite the Foelas Arms Hotel across the river to a car park just beyond the Riverside Chocolate House, with toilets nearby. There is an alternative car park in the village as shown.

*P*entrefoelas *is an attractive estate village built by the Wynne family for its workers and craftsmen. Its water-powered mill was used to ground grain for bread or animal fodder. It was once an important gathering place for cattle and drovers, and in the 19thC a stopping place on Telford's London-Holyhead coach road. The Foelas Arms Hotel, dates from 1762, when its frontage faced east, in 1839 it was enlarged when it took on the licence from a well known coaching house situated at Cernioge 2½ miles to the east. The village is associated with fairies and folklore. One tale involves Huw Llwyd, a famous Welsh sorcerer. While staying here, he was approached by four thieves who thought he was a drover returning from the English market with money. He caused them to be transfixed overnight by a magic horn, which vanished when they were arrested the following morning!*

I Go back towards the A5, then take the signposted path through a small gate on the left just before the bridge. Walk along the field edge near the river. Shortly the waymarked path angles away and rises to a gateway. Go half-LEFT up the next field to a stile by trees and through a small gate above. Angle up the field to cross the ladder-stile ahead – *with views of the mountains of Snowdonia.* Turn LEFT and follow the waymarked path round the field edge to go through a gate. Turn LEFT down a track to go through a gate in the field corner at a signposted path junction.

2 Turn LEFT through an adjoining gate and follow the green track – *part of the original late 18thC London-Holyhead coach road* – to a road junction. Turn RIGHT along the nearby side road signposted to Ysbyty Ifan. After about 150 yards, take the signposted Hiraethog Trail over a ladder-stile on the left. Go up a faint green track, then follow the field edge past a nearby house to a stile/gate in the corner. Go past a large barn to a small gate ahead, then follow a green track up to a stile/gate. Continue up the track, then just before it reaches a gate, turn LEFT with the waymarked path along the field edge to a gate in the corner. Go along the next field edge to a ladder-stile by Plas Iolyn. Go to the end of the barn ahead – *note the stone 'Great Barn' built high up on a rock* – and turn LEFT to pass between outbuildings then the house, and follow its driveway to a road. *Plas Iolyn, with its 18thC wing, was once occupied by the notorious Dr. Ellis Price, a Doctor of Law, whose red robe earned him the name of 'Dr Coch' (Red Doctor) His son, Capt Thomas Price – a seafaring man and poet, along with Capt. Will Myddelton of Denbigh, are said to have been the first men to 'drink' (smoke) tobacco in public in this country.*

3 Turn sharp RIGHT along the road. *Shortly, you will glimpse the 17thC Giler gatehouse. Giler, dating from the 16thC, was once the home of poet Rhys Wynn and the Price family descended from Cardinal Wolsey's cross-bearer.* On the bend, follow the signposted Hiraethog Trail through a gate ahead. Now follow a delightful old enclosed gated green drovers' road for about ¾ mile, skirting the small hill of Bryn Prys. The green track then begins to descend – *with extensive mountain views* – and joins a more defined stony track. (For **Walk B**, then cross a stile on the right and follow the waymarked Hiraethog Trail down to a farm and along its access track to the road. Turn right, then left along a green track and right to rejoin your outward route.)

walks 17 & 18

motte

⑤

Pentrefoelas — A5

A5

N

↑

0   ¼   mile

Walk B

Bryn Prys

Plas Iolyn

walk 18

walk 18

walk 18

②

③

④

LEFT up a stony track. At a track T-junction turn RIGHT and follow the track above a farm and along a field edge to a road.

5 Go along the initially tree-lined driveway opposite, passing Voelas Uchaf, to reach a signposted path junction. *Nearby in the trees are the remains of Foel Las Motte – an earth castle, which once supported a square stone tower, built about 1164.* Turn RIGHT through a gate and follow the track between outbuildings and cottages at Hen Foelas – *site of the original main home of the Wynnes from 1545 to 1819* – then bear left down the narrow track through trees to a kissing gate/gate. Go across the large field towards the end of the wall ahead to another kissing gate. Go down the edge of the next field, through another kissing gate, then follow the field edge round to take a gated

4 Eventually you reach a road. Follow it RIGHT to the entrance to Gwernhywelganol. About 30 yards beyond take an old green track angling left off the bend down to an old facing gate. Follow the remains of a delightful old walled gated green track across upland pasture, then down past woodland to a road/track junction. Follow the road down to cross Pont Newydd over the river Merddwr, to the A5 opposite two cottages. Turn RIGHT along the pavement, then cross the road with care to take the signposted path through a large, then small gate opposite. Go up the field edge by the stream, then at a fence corner follow the waymarked path angling RIGHT across the field up to a small gate in the corner. Go up the next field edge to another small gate near the corner, and turn

path between a large bungalow and a house to the road in Pentrefoelas. Follow it LEFT through the village to the A5 by the Foelas Arms Hotel. Cross the road back to the start.

Foelas Arms Hotel

29

FOEL LAS MOTTE & FFRIDD-Y-FOEL

DESCRIPTION A 5½ mile figure of eight walk through the varied countryside of the Voelas estate, with an old coaching inn or café for refreshments at the end. From Pentrefoelas (see Walk 16 for information) the route follows the Hiraethog Trail past a 12thC earthwork castle, then along a road and green track up to the edge of moorland, reaching a height of 1115 feet/340 metres. It then follows an old drovers' road around the slopes of Ffridd-y-foel, passing an interesting example of estate enterprise, before returning on a choice of routes, featuring a 17thC house. Allow about 3 hours. The route can easily be shortened to a 2 mile walk (**B**), or extended, which I recommend, on a good track with open views across moorland to the remote but attractive Llyn Alwen, adding 4 miles to the distance. (See Walk 19 map).
START Car park, Pentrefoelas [SH 874 514] See Walk 16 for directions. There is an alternative car park in the village as shown.

I Return to the A5 and take the road opposite past the Foelas Arms Hotel through the village, soon bending over the river and passing an old cast iron water pump. Just beyond Hen Ysgol (the old school), turn RIGHT on the signposted Hiraethog Trail gated path between dwellings into a field. Turn LEFT around the field edge up to a kissing gate. Go up the next field edge to another kissing gate, then across the large field to a kissing-gate into a small wood. Follow a stony track up through the trees, then between buildings and dwellings at Hen Voelas to a gate and a signposted path junction beyond. *Only a small altered cottage remains of the original cluster of buildings of Hen Voelas – the original main home of the Wynnes from 1545-1819. Voelas Hall, just over a mile to the west, became the estate home.* Follow the Hiraethog Trail ahead through the wood. *Up to your right is the tree-topped mound of Foel Las Motte. Reputedly made by Owain Gwynedd about 1164, this tall earth castle once supported a*

square stone tower. Its use ceased in 1185. On your left is the remains of a rectangular reservoir. After a gate go along the field edge to a road (For **Walk B** turn left to point 6.)

2 Turn RIGHT along the road, rising steadily up the hillside. After about ½ mile, just after a cattle-grid, turn LEFT on the signposted Hiraethog Trail along a track. Follow it past a small wood and on up to a gate into open upland country. *Pause to enjoy the extensive views of Snowdonia.* Across the valley to the north note the large walled enclosure, which you pass later. Continue up the gated track to a signposted crossroad of paths at the edge of moorland, where you leave the Hiraethog Trail. (For the Llyn Alwen extension, follow the track ahead for 2 miles across moorland, and return the same way.)

3 Turn LEFT and follow a track – *a drovers' road* – across the moorland. It gently descends to ford a stream by a wall/fence. *Upstream is a small waterfall.* Continue up the track to a gate and alongside the large walled enclosure seen earlier. *The high wall is a fine example of dry stone walling. One can only marvel at the skill, patience and time consuming effort that went into its construction in such a wild and inhospitable environment, exposed to the elements. The wall is superior in quality to others nearby. But why? A doorway midway deepens the mystery. A local farmer told me that the enclosure is known as 'The Warren'. It was built for hare-breeding by Voelas estate, presumably at a time when jugged, roast, boiled, potted and hashed hare were culinary delights!*

4 Go through a gate at the enclosure's far end and follow the track alongside the wall through further gates – *enjoying a panorama of mountains from Arenig to the northern Carneddau. Cattle still graze the upland pastures, a reminder of times gone by when animals were fattened on these slopes before being taken by drovers to distant markets.* Later the track descends to a gate. Just beyond go through a gate on the left and descend a walled track towards a

to Llyn Alwen

④ ⑤ ③

N

0   ¼

mile

alternative route

walks 18 & 19

Maes Gwyn

⑥ ②

Foel Las Motte

walk 16

Pentrefoelas   A5

①

walks 16 & 18

along its access track to the road joined earlier. Follow it RIGHT. (For the alternative route shown bear right past the house and through a gate on the left just beyond. Go half-right down the field to a gate near the bottom corner. Turn right along the next field edge, then bear left to cross stepping stones over a river. Follow the line of an old track through a reedy area ahead, soon bearing left along a clearer track to the road by a house. Follow it down to Maes Gwyn and point 6 beyond.

6 At a road junction, a short detour RIGHT will bring you to a fine stone arched bridge over the river and nearby Maes Gwyn dating from 1665. Return along the road and follow it towards Pentrefoelas. Shortly, turn LEFT along a driveway to go past Voelas Uchaf to the signposted path junction at Hen Voelas. Return along your outward route.

farm. After a gate at the bottom, immediately go through another gate on the left. Go alongside the wall above the farmhouse and through a gate in it. Continue with the wall on your left to pass through a gate in the corner. Now head down the field and through a gate near the right-hand corner. Keep ahead across the mid-slope of the next field above telegraph poles to go through a gate onto a track. Continue ahead along it.

5 At a waymarked path junction by the outbuilding of a house you have a choice. For the main route bear LEFT along a green track to a gate, then follow the track down to pass through a farm. Continue

Water pump

31

WALK 18

THE PENTREFOELAS ROUND

DESCRIPTION A 7½ mile (**A**) or 4½ mile (**B**) walk using paths, old coaching and drovers' routes and quiet lanes, through open countryside around Pentrefoelas, with excellent views throughout. The route rises in stages to cross the small hill of Bryn Prys at around 1017 feet/310 metres before descending to pass through 18thC Plas Iolyn, then continuing to the hamlet of Rhydlydan, with its country inn. It then meanders north to join the Hiraethog Trail skirting moorland, reaching a height of 1158 feet/353 metres, before descending with it to Pentrefoelas. Allow about 4½ hours.
START Car park, Pentrefoelas [SH 874514]. See Walk 16 for directions. There is an alternative car park in the village as shown.

I Follow instructions in the first section of Walk 16 for directions.

2 Turn RIGHT along a green track – *part of the original late 18thC London-Holyhead coach road.* At a track junction, follow the track LEFT to a road. Turn RIGHT then soon LEFT up a stony track to follow a waymarked path through Gallt-y-celyn farm. Continue up a green track, soon becoming enclosed, then narrowing to a stile onto a stony track. Follow it LEFT and when it bends right, continue ahead on a green track – *an old drovers' route.*

3 Shortly after a gate, cross a waymarked stile on the left and the wall ahead. Go up the nearby lower gorse covered slope of Bryn Prys, and bear RIGHT, soon crossing the bend of a green track. Continue ahead across a reedy area past a nearby small plantation on the right and through a gate in the wall ahead. Go onto the small ridge to enjoy the panoramic views. Descend the slope towards the right hand corner of the forest below, to join a gated green track. Follow it to the corner of another small plantation ahead. Just

before the stone 'Great Barn' of Plas Iolyn beyond, turn LEFT then bear RIGHT to pass between outbuildings and the house. Follow its driveway to a road. *(See paragraph 2 of Walk 16 for information on Plas Iolyn.)* Follow the road ahead – *a continuation of the earlier drovers' route* – over a crossroad – *the line of a Roman road from Bala to Conwy* – and on to a junction at Rhydlydan. Turn LEFT to the Giler Arms Hotel. *Nearby, in 1820, during construction of Telford's new road (the A5) 40 long-cist graves were uncovered and a 5th/6thC inscribed stone found. It commemorated Brohomaglus Iattus and his wife Caune, and indicated links with Christians in southern Gaul.*

4 Continue along the road – *a section of the old London–Holyhead coach road that Telford's road replaced* – and down to a junction by a 19thC chapel. Here, turn RIGHT along the access track to Pentre Felin. Pass in front of the house and through a gate. Immediately turn RIGHT and go through a waymarked gate then along a field edge. Soon, go through a gate on the right and continue down the next field to a footbridge over the river and up to the A5. Cross the road with care and the stile opposite. Go up the edge of a reedy field to a gate into the old farmyard of Cefngarw. (For **Walk B** turn left and follow an enclosed green track to the A543. Cross the road and follow it left with care, then take a signposted path on the right to pass between a cluster of buildings and on across fields to Pentrefoelas.)

5 For **Walk A** turn RIGHT and follow an old green track for ¹/₃ mile to a gate by a cottage. Follow its access track to the bend of a road. Continue ahead, and at a junction, turn LEFT and follow the road past a cottage to cross a footbridge over a river. At the next junction, follow the road LEFT to the A543 – *now on the Hiraethog Trail.* Turn RIGHT along the road, then LEFT up a side road past a cottage and bungalow. When it bends towards a farm, continue up a waymarked enclosed green track. After a gate, bend RIGHT up a wider enclosed track. *Like the one just left, this is an old drovers' route used to move animals to markets in Denbigh*

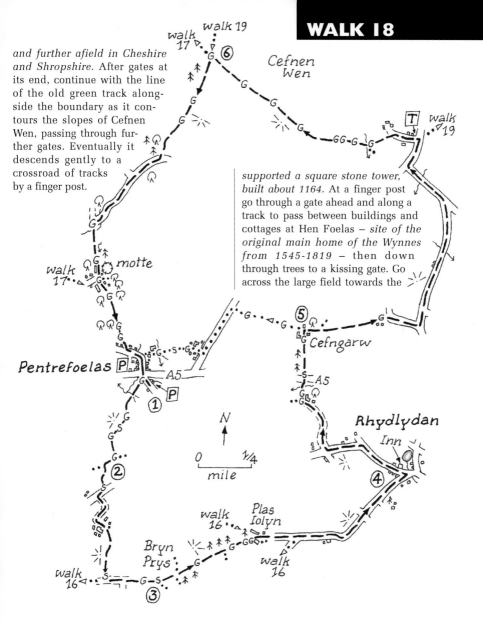

and further afield in Cheshire and Shropshire. After gates at its end, continue with the line of the old green track alongside the boundary as it contours the slopes of Cefnen Wen, passing through further gates. Eventually it descends gently to a crossroad of tracks by a finger post.

walk 17

walk 19

Cefnen Wen

T walk 19

supported a square stone tower, built about 1164. At a finger post go through a gate ahead and along a track to pass between buildings and cottages at Hen Foelas – site of the original main home of the Wynnes from 1545-1819 – then down through trees to a kissing gate. Go across the large field towards the

walk 17

motte

⑤

Cefngarw

Pentrefoelas P

A5

-S- A5

①

P

Rhydlydan

Inn

②

④

N

0   ¼
       mile

Plas Iolyn

walk 16

Bryn Prys

walk 16

walk 16

③

6 Turn LEFT through the gate and follow a delightful gated green track down to a road. Follow it RIGHT for about ½ mile on a steady descent. Just before a cattle grid, go through a kissing gate on the left. Walk along the field edge to a gate and through a wood past a small reservoir. *Up to your left is tree-topped mound of Foel Las Motte, which once* end of the wall ahead to another kissing gate. Go down the edge of the next field, through another kissing gate, then follow the field edge round to take a gated path between a large bungalow and a house to the road in Pentrefoelas. Follow it LEFT through the village to the A5 by the Foelas Arms Hotel. Cross the road back to the start.

WALK 19

THE THREE LAKES TRAIL

DESCRIPTION An exhilarating 10½ mile moorland walk in the heart of Mynydd Hiraethog, visiting three upland lakes of different character – Llyn Aled, the remote natural lake of Llyn Alwen, and the Alwen reservoir. This route requires careful navigation at times and is for the experienced well equipped hill walker who likes wild open moorland. It is best undertaken on a clear sunny day, when the treeless landscape is magical and the panoramic views superb. The initial section to Llyn Alwen is the most demanding, crossing largely pathless and sometimes boggy moorland. It is then followed by a superb 2 mile green track across remote moorland, then a section of the Hiraethog Trail, an old drovers' route. The return follows the route of a medieval road up Bwlch y Garnedd and down to cross the Alwen reservoir for an easy final section along bridleways and road. Allow about 5½ - 6 hours.

START Llyn Aled. [SH 916579].

DIRECTIONS From the A543 Denbigh-Pentrefoelas road take the minor road signposted to Llyn Aled to park by the lake just before it crosses the dam.

1 Follow instructions in the first section of Walk 20.

2 Continue down the path, soon bearing left with a fence down towards the tops of two trees near the right hand end of Llyn Alwen. Later descend via a gate to the old farm of Ty'n-llyn below. *This idyllic location beside the hidden beauty of this remote lake, surrounded by wild and inhospitable moorland makes a gem of a stop on a fine day – a haven of peace and tranquility.* Leave the farm by its green access track alongside the lake edge. After going through a gate you quickly leave the lake behind to follow the delightful green track for 2 miles across the expansive wild moorland. *After the earlier rough crossing it is a pleasure to stride out on this safe passage through such a wild landscape, enjoying the extensive views.*

After going through a second gate there are good views of Moel Hebog, the Nantlle ridge, Snowdon, the Glyders, Tryfan and the Carneddau. Eventually the track reaches a signposted crossroad of paths at a track junction just before a gate.

3 Turn LEFT on the waymarked Hiraethog Trail and follow an old gated green track – variable in quality – alongside a wall, contouring the mid-slopes of Cefnen Wen. *This is an old drovers' route used to move animals to markets in Denbigh and further afield in Cheshire and Shropshire.* After a double set of gates, the track becomes enclosed and begins to descend. About 100 yards after passing through another gate, at the broadest section of the track, bear LEFT through a waymarked gate. Now follow another enclosed track to descend past a farm, and continue down its access road past a cottage and bungalow to the A543. Go through the waymarked gate opposite, then go half-LEFT to cross a footbridge over a stream. Continue up the slope ahead to follow a wide enclosed track past farm buildings to go through a second gate into open country.

4 Continue ahead alongside the old wall to join and follow an enclosed track, soon bending half-LEFT. After going through a gate, keep with this delightful, but steadily deteriorating track, as it rises gently across open upland pasture. Go through a gate just above the track and continue ahead to pass a small ruin. Continue along the line of the old track. *Note the many lichen-covered stones.* At a more distinct cross track, turn RIGHT and soon follow the line of the old embanked Pentrefoelas-Denbigh road rising up Bwlch y Garnedd. *This ancient road fell out of use after the building of the turnpike road, now the A543, in 1826.* After passing a large squat stone, continue with a clear path along the right side of the old road to reach the top of the bwlch. *Up to the right is the cairned top of heather covered Mwdwl-eithin. A boulder near the top of the pass makes a good place for a break to enjoy the views, soon to disappear. From the top of the bwlch can be seen Llyn Aled and Llyn Alwen.* Follow a path across the reedy moorland, where little

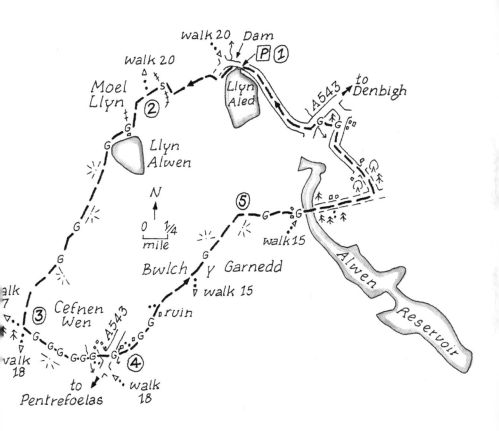

remains of the old road, to go through a gate in the fence ahead. Continue on the line of the old track as it contours north east across tussocky/reedy ground.

5 At a good view of Alwen reservoir, the old track goes half-RIGHT and descends to a gate, then continues down the hillside – *enjoying panoramic views of Alwen reservoir en route –* to reach a tree by the small ruin of Nant Heilyn – *the former home of Heilyn, an 18thC highwayman, whose hoard of stolen silver and gold may still lie hidden nearby!* Go past nearby sheepfolds to join the Alwen Trail at a bridge over the stream. Follow it to cross a long footbridge over the neck of the reservoir. Continue up a stony track (a bridleway), soon leaving the Alwen Trail, past the house of Pen-y-ffrith, and keep with the track for about ½ mile. At a signposted bridleway junction, turn LEFT along another track, shortly descending past the entrance to Hafod Elwy Hall and the large stone outbuilding of Tan-y-graig farm. Continue with the access track, then at the next farm, go through a gate on the left opposite a barn. Go past a small plantation and follow the fence round to a gate above a stream to reach the A543. Cross the road and follow it LEFT, then take the road back to Llyn Aled. *The expansive beauty of the lake makes an enjoyable finale to the walk.*

WALK 20

MOEL LLYN

DESCRIPTION An exhilarating 8½ mile walk exploring the expansive area of moorland and upland pasture in the northern part of Mynydd Hiraethog near Llyn Aled and Isaf Aled reservoirs, offering extensive views. The route crosses moorland to a great viewpoint on Moel Llyn, before heading north. It then follows a delightful upland track via Llys Dymper and a section of the North Wales Pilgrim's Way, before returning by Foel Lwyd, then road past Aled Isaf. This route is for experienced hill walkers, for its outward route to point 3 crosses wild moorland, boggy in parts, requiring careful navigation. It should be avoided in poor visibility. Allow about 4½ hours.

START Llyn Aled [SH 916579].

DIRECTIONS From the A543 Denbigh-Pentrefoelas road take the minor road signposted to Llyn Aled to park by the lake corner just before it bends left.

1 Follow the road past the castellated stone building that controls the outflow from Llyn Aled – *built in 1934 as a regulating reservoir*. On the bend follow a track ahead. At a gate/stile turn RIGHT up a narrow reedy track, soon bending left. Just beyond an old embanked boundary, when the track angles left, continue along a path ahead. After a few yards, take its right fork. Soon continue along its lower right fork along the left hand side of a shallow moorland valley, passing on the higher ground to your right, a tree/hedge boundary, then a small stone sheepfold. When the path bends left continue ahead across the tussocky moorland to reach a visible wooden corner of a fence ahead by an old inscribed Hiraethog slate boundary stone. Turn RIGHT alongside the fence up to cross a stile in it on the rise after about 300 yards. Go slightly RIGHT for about 200 yards onto higher ground ahead to enjoy the extensive views of the mountains of Snowdonia. Look for a clear cross-path and follow it LEFT (south westwards), briefly descending then rising to the inauspicious top of Moel Llyn ahead – *with a view down to Llyn Alwen.*

2 Return along the path and follow it north to a gate in the fence crossed earlier. Work your way northwards across the wide expanse of tussocky moorland, aiming for the right end of a distant grass ridge. After crossing higher ground ahead continue parallel with the fence on your left across drier terrain, moving closer to it to pick up a path. After crossing a reedy wet area near the fence follow it up the slope ahead, past sheepfolds and down to a gate in the corner.

3 Go through the gate and another across a track below. Follow it up to a gate and on to a track junction on Llys Dymper – *with a panoramic view to Snowdonia.* Turn RIGHT and follow the delightful gated track across the expansive plateau. After about 1 mile, the track begins a long steady descent, passes a derelict cottage and becomes a road. Follow it down to a cross-path, where you join the North Wales Pilgrims Way. Turn RIGHT over a stile, then go down the field and through a gate below a derelict cottage, and left through another. Bear RIGHT along a track, through gates, over a stream and up to a gate. The old reedy track now rises steadily near a stream to another gate. Continue ahead near the stream, then bend LEFT through reeds and up the field edge beneath the fence. After passing below sheepfolds, follow a narrow green track ahead to the road.

4 Turn RIGHT up it past Tynyffynnon, then take the signposted path up the access track to Tai'n-y-foel. Go through a gate on the right, then up the long field edge to a gate in the corner. Keep ahead across Foel Lwyd's wide moorland top then join the fence on the left down to the road by a ruined cottage. Follow it RIGHT, soon descending to cross the dam of Aled Isaf – *a regulating reservoir built in the 1930s* – by an impressive gorge containing Rhaeadr y Bedd waterfall. *During 1974, low water levels revealed evidence of mesolithic hunter/gatherers, who roamed through this area when a gentler climate and woodland habitat made it a less hostile environment.* Continue with the road back to Llyn Aled.

WALK 21
BRYN POETH

DESCRIPTION A 5 mile undulating upland walk, featuring a 'Big Sky' and extensive views. The route heads south across remote upland pasture and moorland, crossing Bryn Poeth (1443 feet/440 metres), before returning on a delightful track past Llys Dymper and across an upland plateau, then a short section of the North Wales Pilgrim's Way. Allow about 3 hours. Avoid in poor visibility.
START Bend of minor road [SH 909618]
DESCRIPTION The side road lies 3 miles south of Llansannan and 1¼ miles north of Aled Isaf, opposite Gors Llyn Gwyn. There is limited vergeside parking before the bend.

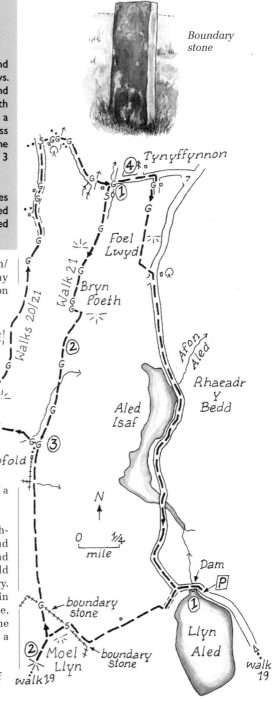

Boundary stone

1 On the bend take the signposted path/ waymarked North Wales Pilgrim's Way to a stile/gate. Follow the reedy track, soon bending up between banks of gorse. Just before it enters the field turn LEFT up the slope to a stile ahead. Go up the field edge, past the fence corner and on above the stream to a gate, then up the middle of the next long field to another gate. Continue ahead across moorland to go through a gate, then another on the left about 25 yards beyond. onto the nearby small flat tussocky top of Bryn Poeth – *enjoying extensive all-round views*. Now head south, parallel with the fence on your right, down to the corner of a fenced embanked boundary ahead.

2 Walk beside it to a low gate in another boundary corner. Continue ahead between an old embanked boundary and a fence, over a stream, and on to an old gate at the end of the embanked boundary. Go ahead across the reedy/tussocky terrain towards a fence by a cleft on the skyline, soon above the reedy stream, to join the incoming fence on your right. Follow it to a gate in its corner.

3 Follow instructions in paragraph 3 of Walk 20 back to the start.

WALK 22
AROUND CWM CLEDWEN

DESCRIPTION A 6 mile walk (**A**) exploring the hills on both sides of the Cledwen valley in which lies the remote ancient community of Gwytherin. It offers extensive views, especially of the Snowdonia mountains. The route rises steadily to upland pasture, reaching a height of 1312 feet/410 metres, before descending back into Cwm Cledwen. It then climbs an attractive side valley and crosses an expansive moorland plateau, reaching a height of over 1345 feet/400 metres, before descending with a section of the North Wales Pilgrim's Way to Gwytherin. Allow about 4 hours. The route can be shortened to a 5 mile walk (**B**) or by utilising the quiet valley road, can be undertaken as two separate walks of 4½ miles (**C**) and 4 miles (**D**).
START Gwytherin [SH 876615].
DIRECTIONS Gwytherin lies 4 miles south west of Llansannan on the B5384. Park tidily in the village centre.

*G*wytherin has an important ecclesiastical past. St Winifred's church, was built in 1869 to replace an earlier one. Legend has it that St Winifred, associated with the 'holy well' in Holywell, later came to Gwytherin, where she became abbess at a local nunnery in the 12thC. After her death her remains were kept in the former church, but were eventually transferred to Shrewsbury. The churchyard contains old yew trees, and a line of four small standing stones. One, dating from the 5th/6thC and inscribed in Latin, commemorates Vinnemaglus. Such stones provided the earliest evidence of Christianity. In the village centre on the site of a former smithy is a plaque to one of its famous sons, Clwydfardd (1800-94), the first Archdruid. The nearby Lion Inn is now a guesthouse.

I (For **Walk C** follow the road south to join the main route at point 3.) For the main walk, at the village road junction, turn RIGHT signposted to Llansannan then RIGHT again along the 'No through road'.

Follow it past the community centre, over the Afon Cledwen and on through Dol-fadyn farm. Continue up the road to its end a gate at Bryn-y-clochydd farm. Just beyond go up the left fork of a stony track to a gate to begin a long steady climb up a concrete then stony track. After a gate at a good viewpoint bear LEFT to another gate and continue up the stony track, later levelling out.

2 When the track heads half-left, go through a gate ahead. Go across the upland pasture of Pen Bryn y Clochydd to a gate, then across part-reedy terrain to another gate ahead. Bear RIGHT to follow a reedy stream down to the former cottage of Pant-y-fotty. Cross the stream to a small iron gate, then go across the slope to join a green track, passing through two gates by a sheepfold. The track heads west – *with views south into the heart of Mynydd Hiraethog*. When the track splits bear LEFT to a gate. Beyond leave the track and go half-RIGHT to descend a short old narrow sunken green track. Bear RIGHT across the end of a descending track to a gate ahead. Go across the next field, parallel with the fence on your right, towards the panorama of mountains of Snowdonia. After about 200 yards, bear LEFT to join a narrow green track beneath a small knoll to a gate. Continue ahead, soon descending steadily to follow the fence below down to a gate its corner. Now follow an improving green track down the hillside by the old embanked boundary, shortly bending down to ford a stream and continuing past a footbridge to Tu-hwnt-ir-afon. Cross a ladder-stile by the first building, then follow the field edge past the house to cross a stile in the corner and a footbridge over the Afon Cledwyn. Turn RIGHT along the road. (For **Walk D** follow it all the way along the valley to Gwytherin)

3 After ¼ mile turn up the driveway to Tai Pellaf. After passing the first large barn, turn RIGHT and go through a gate by a stream. Now follow a stony track up the attractive side valley. After ⅓ mile, keep with the main track between a fork angling down left and another just beyond doing a sharp u-turn right, to cross a confluence of streams and rising LEFT to a track junction. Bend RIGHT to follow the reedy track up the left hand side of the narrow valley to a gate, and on up reedy upland pasture track to a gate onto a road. Follow it RIGHT, and after about 250 yards go through a gate on your left opposite another – *with a good view of nearby wind turbines.* (For **Walk B** follow the road down to join the valley road to Gwytherin). Go across upland pasture to a gate in the fence ahead. Angle 30° LEFT through reeds and across pasture for about 150 yards to a waymarked stile near a fence corner. Now follow the fence on your left on a long gentle ascent across moorland – *enjoying extensive views* – to a gate. Continue beside the fence.

4 Go past a waymarked stile and follow the fence along the moorland edge to a wide track. Follow it RIGHT, soon steadily descending to cross a stream and pass a gated side track. After a stile/gate the track descends towards the old cottage of Pen-y-graig. Just before it cross a stile up on the right. Pass behind the building and go down to another stile beyond. Keep ahead down the edge of upland pasture above a narrow wooded side valley. Shortly pass to the left of a large area of gorse down to the top end of an old tree-topped embanked boundary. Keeping the boundary on your left follow it down through trees, soon joining a good path descending the edge of the wooded valley, moving steadily closer to the stream below. Cross a stile and follow the stream down to Pentre, its access track, then a path by the stream to the road in Gwytherin.

View towards the mountains of Snowdonia

PRONUNCIATION

These basic points should help non-Welsh speakers

Welsh	English equivalent
c	always hard, as in cat
ch	as in the Scottish word loch
dd	as th in then
f	as v in vocal
ff	as f
g	always hard as in got
ll	no real equivalent. It is like 'th' in then, but with an 'L' sound added to it, giving **'thlan'** for the pronunciation of the Welsh 'Llan'.

In Welsh the accent usually falls on the last-but-one syllable of a word.

KEY TO THE MAPS

- ➔ Walk route and direction
- ═ Metalled road
- ▬ Unsurfaced road
- •••• Footpath/route adjoining walk route
- ∿ River/stream
- ♣ ♤ Trees
- ▬▬ Railway
- **G** Gate
- **S** Stile
- **F.B.** Footbridge
- ⊻ Viewpoint
- [P] Parking
- [T] Telephone
- 🚐 Caravan site

Published by
Kittiwake Books Limited
3 Glantwymyn Village Workshops, Glantwymyn,
Machynlleth, Montgomeryshire SY20 8LY

© Text & map research: David Berry 2017
© Maps & illustrations: Kittiwake 2017
First edition 2001; Second edition: 2007
Illustrations by Morag Perrott
Cover photographs: *Main:* Cwm Merddwr (Walk
16); *Inset:* Alwen reservoir dam (Walk 9)

Care has been taken to be accurate. However
neither the author nor the publisher can accept
responsibility for any errors which may appear, or
their consequences. If you are in doubt about any
path, check before you start out.

Printed by Mixam, UK.
ISBN: 978 1 908748 42 3

THE COUNTRY CODE

- Be safe – plan ahead and follow any signs
- Leave gates and property as you find them
- Protect plants and animals, and take your litter home
- Keep dogs under close control
- Consider other people

Open Access
Some routes cross areas of land where walkers have
the legal right of access under The CRoW Act 2000.
Open Access land is detailed on OS Explorer 264
and OL18 maps which cover this area. Access can
be subject to restrictions and closure for up to 28
days a year. Please respect any notices.

Useful contacts
Denbighshire County Council's Rights of Way:
www.denbighshire.gov.uk or 01824 706101.
Conwy Council's Rights of Way: www.conwy.gov.uk
or 01492 575546

About the author, David Berry

David is an experienced walker with a love of
the countryside and an interest in local history.
He is the author of a series of walks guidebooks
covering North Wales, where he has lived and
worked for many years. He has written for
Walking Wales and Ramblers Walk magazine,
worked as a Rights of Way surveyor across North
Wales and served as a member of Denbighshire
Local Access Forum.
For more information visit
www.davidberrywalks.co.uk